The Origins of the

Middle Ages

Historical Controversies · A Norton Series

Under the general editorship of BRYCE LYON, *Brown University*

This series has been developed in response to the growing interest in historical interpretation, in the how and why of history as opposed to pure narrative accounts. Each volume discusses a major historical problem with analysis of the leading interpretations past and present.

The Origins of the

Middle Ages

PIRENNE'S CHALLENGE TO GIBBON

by Bryce Lyon

Brown University

W · W · Norton & Company · Inc · New York

FIRST EDITION

Library of Congress Catalog Card No. 77–163374

SBN 393 05449 7 Cloth Edition
SBN 393 09993 8 *Paper Edition*

1 2 3 4 5 6 7 8 9 0

Contents

Preface

This essay is essentially a study in historiography, concerned with what historians and thinkers have considered the principal reasons for the end of the ancient world and the beginning of the Middle Ages. To learn what has been said on this problem is also to gain insights into the thinking, the problems, the methodology, the attitudes, the philosophies, and the ideas on the nature of evidence and truth of such historians since the time of the Roman Empire as St. Augustine, Machiavelli, Edward Gibbon, and Henri Pirenne. Historiography is in essence a study of the thought of past historical ages.

Although history became a discipline or profession only during the nineteenth century and although most of the scholarly writing on the decline of the ancient world has been done during the nineteenth and twentieth centuries, to limit this essay to an evaluation of historical writing since Edward Gibbon's time would eliminate Machiavelli, Voltaire, Montesquieu, and others whose writing on this problem has been seminal and remains influential. They have therefore been included. Study of late classical, Renaissance, Reformation, and Enlightenment historiography underscores the great debt of modern historians to their distant predecessors, of modern thought to that of previous ages, even the Middle Ages.

The scholarly paraphernalia that too often decorates the bottoms of pages and frequently bores or paralyzes both scholar and student has been kept to a minimum in this essay. Notes appear in the text only when essential. A comprehensive bibliography at the end of the text lists in alphabetical order the authors discussed or cited with the titles of their works in the best and latest editions, as well as those available in paperback. For the sake of convenience, page references are given in the bibliography, indicating discussion of the work in the text. Occasionally, other pertinent writings on historiography or on the lives of some of the historians are included. To give some idea of chronology, dates are inserted for the principal historians writing prior to the publication of Henri Pirenne's *Mahomet et Charlemagne* in 1937, but not for those writing in the thirty-odd years since. The interested reader can easily find the dates for their works in the bibliography.

Introduction

Why have brilliant civilizations flowered and then declined? Why have some states become powerful and then suddenly disintegrated? Why have others attained only the level of survival? Why at various times in certain areas of the world has there been magnificent artistic and intellectual achievement, then later a withering of it, with men losing the ability to innovate and to think creatively? Why have efficient and dynamic economies abruptly become sick and incapable of supporting society and the state? And why, after centuries of stability, have societies collapsed?

Many talented historians and philosophers have wrestled with such problems. The nature of the good state and its preservation preoccupied Greek philosophers such as Plato and Aristotle. In the *History of the Persian Wars,* Herodotus (*ca.* 484–424 B.C.) sought to explain how a group of tiny Greek city-states could halt the westward expansion of the great Persian Empire. Was he right in believing that it was because of Greek cultural superiority over barbarians (his term for all non-Greeks including the Persians)? In his sophisticated and probing *History of the Peloponnesian War,* Thucydides (*ca.* 471–400 B.C.) is concerned with how Athens, the most creative politically and culturally of all the Greek city-states, could be humbled by a militaristic and authoritarian Sparta. He develops the theme that the Athenians were brought to their knees through arrogance and their ultimate belief in the doctrine that might makes right. Studying the Roman Republic, the Greek historian Polybius (*ca.* 205–125 B.C.) tried to ascertain why Roman political institutions were so stable while those of

Greece were so prone to civil war and particularism. He was convinced that the Roman Republic had escaped the cycle of continual and violent change from tyranny to kingship, aristocracy, oligarchy, democracy, and back to tyranny that he had observed in Greek political life by achieving a balance of power between the various classes and organs of government. Roman historians, less probing and philosophical than the Greeks, wondered why the Roman Republic, after five centuries of growth and durable government, should disintegrate and be replaced by imperial authority. Tacitus found his answer in the moral degeneration of the Roman aristocracy which, losing its drive and sense of civic and military obligation, surrendered its position and authority to the emperors who saddled the state with tyranny.

Centuries later the English historian Edward Gibbon (1737–1794), like so many later historians, sought an answer to why the ancient world in the form of the majestic Roman Empire declined in the West, yielding its place to the Germans, and thereby inaugurating a long and quite different historical period known as the Middle Ages that gave root to a new civilization. "It was at Rome," he wrote, "on the fifteenth of October 1764, as I sat musing amidst the ruins of the Capitol while the barefooted fryars were singing Vespers in the temple of Jupiter, that the idea of writing the decline and fall of the City first started to my mind." [1] It is not surprising that Gibbon, steeped in classical history and literature, should write on Roman history, but to focus on the decline and fall of the Roman Empire, a problem most historians consider one of the most fundamental and difficult of western history, is indicative of his extraordinary intellectual endowment.

That Gibbon's history of the Roman Empire from the Antonines to the fall of the Byzantine capital Constantinople in 1453 remained supreme for many years attests to his achievement. Only recently have historians discussed the end of the ancient world and the beginning of the Middle Ages in other than the historical perspective and terms of Gibbon. Because his history was the first systematic and scholarly treatment of this problem, it is a watershed. This great work, however, represents but one phase in historians' long and continuing debate on Rome's decline. To comprehend how

1. Bonnard, *Edward Gibbon, Memoirs of My Life,* p. 136.

and when the ancient world ended necessitates knowing what historians thought prior to Gibbon, understanding his interpretation and its influence upon historians of the nineteenth and twentieth centuries, and realizing that since World War I, historians have rejected much of his interpretation and advanced radically different arguments and solutions.

Chronology

509 B.C.–27 B.C.	Roman Republic
27 B.C.–A.D. 14	Rule of first Roman emperor Augustus
180	Death of the Roman emperor Marcus Aurelius
235–284	Civil war in the Roman Empire
284–305	Rule of the Roman emperor Diocletian
306–337	Rule of the Roman emperor Constantine
311	Constantine's edict of toleration for Christianity
330	Constantinople becomes the capital of the Roman Empire
354–430	St. Augustine, author of *City of God*
395	Death of Thedosius I, last emperor to rule over eastern and western parts of the Roman Empire
350–600	Germanic penetration of the West
410	Visigoths pillage Rome
455	Vandals pillage Rome
476	Deposition of the last Roman emperor Romulus Augustulus by the German leader Odoacer
481–511	Rule of Clovis, first Merovingian king of the Franks
527–565	Rule of Justinian, emperor of the Eastern Roman Empire
570–632	Mohammed
639–750	Arab conquests around the Mediterranean Sea
674–677	Arab siege of Constantinople
732	Defeat of Arabs by Charles Martel at Tours
751	Deposition of last Merovingian king and accession of Pepin the Short, first Carolingian king of the Franks
768–814	Rule of Charlemagne, king of the Franks
800	Coronation of Charlemagne at Rome as emperor of the Holy Roman Empire
814–887	Disintegration of the Carolingian Empire
900–1000	Stabilization of western Europe

1. Gibbon and Before

EARLY CHRISTIAN ATTACKS AND
THE HOLY ROMAN EMPIRE

Each generation of historians has approached the problem from the historical experience of its own age. It is perhaps true, as one historian has written, that the answers to this problem "form a commentary upon the ages that proposed them." [2] But Rome's decline did not become a topical question of history until about five hundred years ago during the Renaissance, when men saw themselves as living in an age unlike the previous nine or ten centuries and saw these centuries as totally different from the ancient world.

Throughout the imperial period there were men who felt that the social structure, the institutions, and the ideals of Rome were deteriorating. The fourth-century Roman historian Lactantius relates how the Stoic philosopher Seneca complained even in the first century A.D. that Rome had become aged and could anticipate only a slow death. Although other Stoics concurred, not until the growth of Christianity did Rome's decline become an issue of debate. According to the Book of Revelation, the Roman Empire would be destroyed and there would follow the millennium and the Day of Last Judgment. The Christian fathers of the fourth and fifth centuries continually repeated this theme, especially when the Germans, an increasing menace pushing into the heart of the empire, occupied and pillaged the Eternal City itself in 410. Typical of the Christians who regarded these events as divine

2. Walbank, *The Decline of the Roman Empire in the West*, p. 1.

punishment for Rome's long history of sin, St. Jerome attacked Rome as a center of harlots, an empire that must be
destroyed because its haughty rulers "deem it eternal."

While Christian writers were reviling Rome for her paganism and immoral behavior and interpreting the imperial troubles as a prelude to ultimate destruction, a time of Last
Judgment, and a replacement by God's kingdom, they also had
to defend Christianity against pagan intellectuals who, in the
face of Roman military and political disasters, blamed it for
Rome's troubles. With their belief in Rome's eternity an un-
challenged article of faith, most pagans were shocked by
Roman reversals and began to ask whether "Rome had per-
ished in Christian times." Some were certain that the troubles
stemmed from neglect of the ancient pagan rites. Others, like
the fifth-century Volusianus, posed the essential question of
whether the precept of turning the other cheek to the smiter
could be reconciled with a strong state that owed its success
to war and might, whether Christianity was therefore not the
cause of Rome's decadence.

Stung by such accusations, the Christians, led by St. Augustine (354–430), launched a counteroffensive. The source
for decay of the Roman state, wrote St. Augustine, could be
found long before Christ in the degeneration of old Roman
morality, in the rise of venality, licence, and crime, all con-
doned by the pagan gods. What were Roman conquests, ex-
ecuted without justice, other than brigandage on a huge scale?
This theme of St. Augustine, most evident in the *Civitas Dei,*
was soon buttressed by the Spanish priest Orosius in his *Seven
Books Against the Pagans.* Arriving at St. Augustine's Hippo
in North Africa from Spain, which had been overrun by the
Sueves and Vandals, Orosius was persuaded by St. Augustine
to refute the pagan assertion that Rome's decline was caused
by abandonment of her old gods. Acknowledging that St.
Augustine had bade him reply to "the empty chatter and per-
versity" of the pagans, he then wrote a history of Rome show-
ing that "the days of the past were not only as oppressive as
those of the present but that they were the more terribly
wretched the further they were removed from the consolation
of true religion." [3] So were drawn the lines between pagan
and Christian, so were propounded some of the arguments

3. Orosius, *Seven Books Against the Pagans,* pp. 29–31.

adopted by later historians. Emerging as the principal Christian theme is that God does not promise eternity to anything earthly, that only the Spiritual City, the *Civitas Dei,* is eternal and, without frontiers, embraces all peoples and all the faithful on both sides of the river of death.

To avoid ambiguity over the Christian position it must be understood that all Christians regarded the empire as temporal, as the earthly city, and that in the future, on the Day of Last Judgment, it would end and be replaced by the eternal City of God. None believed or stated, however, that it was in the process of disappearing within a few years or that it had already ceased to exist; for them the imperial death was a future event that would come with the millennium. St. Augustine, in fact, justified the existence of the Roman Empire as a political and social necessity, an institution to protect sinful man from lawlessness, disorder, and killing until the advent of the City of God. He saw conventional man-made government as God's appointed remedy for sin, and therefore justified in its use of force to repress sin. Although doomed ultimately to destruction, this government, which recently had become Christian, was to be preserved until the coming of the City of God because it upheld and enforced the true faith by which all men were saved. James Bryce was correct in arguing that the theory of the Holy Roman Empire derived from St. Augustine's City of God.

Both pagan and Christian regarded the fourth and fifth centuries as a time of profound troubles, of crisis, but not as a time when the empire had died. In the following turbulent centuries there is no evidence that anyone believed an age or empire had ended and a new age had begun. Under the influence of St. Augustine and Orosius, medieval writers pictured the Roman Empire as the last of the four great world monarchies, the one that would continue until the advent of the City of God. They agreed with St. Augustine that the pagan Roman Empire had become Christian, that although this transition had occurred long before Charlemagne, his coronation as emperor of the Romans by Pope Leo III on Christmas Day 800 in the basilica of St. Peter at Rome symbolized this transition from Roman Empire to Holy Roman Empire. Throughout the Middle Ages the fiction held that this event marked the *translatio imperii ad Francos* or *ad Teutonicos.*

No medieval writer could perceive a distinction between the Roman Empire or the ancient world and the age that followed. Such medieval historians as Otto, bishop of Freising (1114?–1158), realized that the pagan Roman Empire had declined but considered this only a symptom of an aging world moving toward its death. Even in the early fourteenth century when Dante wrote the *De Monarchia* the belief was that, although continually declining, a universal empire, now Christian, still existed.

RENAISSANCE WRITERS AND THE DECLINE

Not until the stirring of the Italian Renaissance in the late fourteenth century when western Europe truly awoke to the magnificent cultural achievements of the Greeks and Romans, did humanists begin to view the age in which they lived as different from the centuries just preceding and to view those centuries as quite different from what they came to call the ancient world. There arose the desire to understand why the brilliant classical civilization so admired and so copied by Renaissance men withered and gave way to a thousand years of Gothic darkness. With these humanists of the fourteenth century, therefore, the end of the ancient world and the beginning of the Middle Ages became a historical problem, a past event that needed explanation.

Living in the highly politicized atmosphere of the Italian city-state and often participating in city-state affairs, most humanists naturally sought political and military explanations for Rome's fall. One of the first to suggest an answer typical of many during the fourteenth, fifteenth, and sixteenth centuries was Petrarch (1304–1374). An enthusiastic admirer of the Roman Republic, he praised Brutus and Pompey as defenders of republican virtue and liberty and damned Julius Caesar as the real culprit for Rome's troubles because he destroyed liberty and introduced one-man rule. With the contemporary Florentine historian Giovanni Villani (1280?–1348), Petrarch saw the Roman Empire as ending at a particular point in time. But while Villani asserted that the Roman Empire was overwhelmed by the German barbarians,

Petrarch, agreeing that the Germans were a primary cause for the destruction of Rome, ascribed the real division between ancient and later history to the advent of the Christian-barbarian era. He called ancient (*antiqua*) that period of history prior to the adoption of Christianity by such emperors as Constantine and Theodosius in the fourth century, and modern (*nova*) that period from the fourth century to his own age, a period he regarded as one of barbarism and darkness (*tenebrae*). He was the first to conceive of the period from the end of the ancient world to the fourteenth century as the Dark Ages, an interpretation accepted by most historians until the last quarter of the nineteenth century. By arguing that barbarism and the triumph of Christianity ended the Roman Empire, he logically could accept no *imperium* except that of the Romans and had therefore to reject the *translatio imperii* to the Holy Roman Empire. Agreeing with Petrarch that the decline of republican political liberty and morals came with the imperial period, Leonardo Bruni (1369–1444) wrote in his *History of the Florentine People* that "the Roman imperium began to go to ruin when first the name of Caesar fell like a disaster upon the city." [4] It was, he believed, inevitable that the degenerate Romans should collapse under the barbarian invasions. The Roman Empire in the West ended when the western provinces were occupied by the Germans and when Constantine moved the imperial capital to Byzantium on the Bosphorus, renaming it Constantinople. Like Petrarch, he totally rejected the fiction of the *translatio imperii*.

As the Italian humanists became more engrossed in their study of the Graeco-Roman world and more confident in their knowledge of the past, they tried to be more precise in their chronology. In his *History from the Decline of the Roman Empire* (1439–1453) the papal secretary, Flavio Biondo, dated the fall of the Roman Empire with the sack of Rome by Alaric and the Visigoths in 410 and interpreted the next thousand years as a middle period shrouded in darkness. Machiavelli modeled the historical conceptualization of his *Florentine History* (1525) upon that of Bruni and Biondo. Beginning with the barbarian invasions that marked the end of Rome, he continued his account to the accession of the Medici in 1434.

4. Bruni, *Historiarum Florentini Populi Libri XII*, p. 14.

From Polybius, to whom he owed much of his knowledge of Republican Rome, he borrowed the cyclical view, transferring it almost into a law of nature responsible for the continuous process of rise and decline in history. He argued "that valor produces peace; peace, repose; repose, disorder; disorder, ruin; so from disorder order springs; from order virtue; and from this glory and good fortune." [5] Like Petrarch, Machiavelli explained the barbarian triumph over the empire by the deterioration of civic virtue and military ardor and also used contemporary Italian politics and war to explain the Roman debacle. Barbarian invasions had to be a prime cause of Rome's fall when for centuries the Italian city-states had been victimized and the Italian peninsula wracked with disunity because of repeated invasions of Italy by German and French forces. Endemic civil war and unstable political regimes within the city-states served to substantiate his belief in political cycles derived from Polybius.

In accord that a combination of political and military disasters caused Rome's fall early in the fifth century, Italian humanists interested in classical culture and art buttressed this interpretation by ascribing the destruction of classical culture to the barbarians. Biondo saw a gradual degeneration in Latin letters after Cicero, climaxed by their death in the fifth century. There were few in the wake of the church fathers Ambrose, Jerome, and Augustine who could write elegant Latin. This view, echoed by other writers such as Paolo Cortese in his *Dialogue of Learned Men* (1490), was reflected by Renaissance artists and art critics. In his second *Commentary* which appeared in the mid-fifteenth century, Ghiberti (1378–1455) avowed that ancient art degenerated at the time of Constantine and that painting and other arts revived only with Cimabue and Giotto in the late thirteenth century. Giorgio Vasari in his famous *Lives of the Most Eminent Painters, Sculptors, and Architects* (1550) likewise made Constantine the boundary between the good art of the ancient world and the dismal art that immediately followed. After an artistic awakening in the second half of the thirteenth century with Cimabue and Giotto, artists "purged their minds of the grossness of the past" and became able to "distinguish between

5. Machiavelli, *History of Florence and of the Affairs of Italy from the Earliest Times to the Death of Lorenzo the Magnificent,* p. 204.

what was good and what was bad" and imitated "the works of antiquity." [6]

This view of literature and art was adopted north of the Alps, especially by the French humanists. In 1559, for example, Jacques Amyot in dedicating his translation of Plutarch to King Henry II of France reminded him that his father Francis I "happily founded good letters and made them to be reborn (*renaistre*) and to flourish in this noble kingdom." [7] As the concept of *rinascita* had taken over in Italy, so the *renaissance des lettres* came to France.

OPINION IN NORTHERN EUROPE

For the learned Erasmus (1466?–1536), who dated the end of good Latin letters with the last of the Christian fathers after whom not only Latin but the Christian faith was barbarized, the enemy was arid scholasticism which induced barbarization of religion, art, and letters. In his *Book Against the Barbarians* (1520) he asserted that the real barbarians, the real Goths, were actually the monks and schoolmen who destroyed good theology and learning. Philip Melanchthon (1497–1560) followed the analysis of Erasmus except that he associated the extinction of classical learning with the Gothic and Lombard invasions.

While Italian and French humanists heaped abuse upon the Germans for destroying Rome and for causing a thousand years of Gothic darkness, German humanists, defensive about their ancestors, interpreted their role quite differently. They agreed that the Germans ended one age and ushered in another but, like Johannes Nauclerus in his *Chronicles of All Ages and of All Memorable Peoples* (1516), praised them for injecting their blood and vigor into western Europe during their *Völkerwanderung*. Nauclerus cited the coronation of Charlemagne as evidence of the divinely ordained superiority of the Germans and agreed with medieval writers that there had been a *translatio imperii* to the Germans in the

6. Vasari, *The Lives of the Most Eminent Painters, Sculptors, and Architects*, p. 45.

7. Amyot, *Les vies des hommes illustres . . . par Plutarque*, I, a, iii.

person of Charlemagne. While seeing the Germans as introducing a new phase of western European history, German
humanists, choosing to avoid the position of damning their
past history, were loath to relate the Germans with a line of
demarcation between the ancient world and what followed.
Psychologically incapable of admitting that their ancestors destroyed classical culture, they concentrated upon proving a
continuity in German history and upon glorifying German
accomplishments which, in their eyes, took on heroic propor-
tions after the end of the Roman Empire in the West.

On the eve of the Reformation, then, we see humanists,
both southern and northern, agreeing that the essential character of the ancient world disappeared in the fourth and fifth
centuries, yielding to a society quite different politically,
socially, culturally, and spiritually, but disagreeing as to the
effect of this change. German humanists could not admit that
the change was bad, while the others insisted that it was a
catastrophe and attributed it to a combination of the moral,
civic, and military degeneration of the Romans and the barbarian invasions. There was as yet only a hint that the Christian religion was also responsible.

With the coming of the Reformation, Protestant historians
agreed with the humanists that the ancient world ended in
the fifth century but advanced a new explanation, derived
more from divine inspiration than from human causes. Their
theme was that the pure evangelical doctrine of the early
Christian church had been deformed by the Roman Catholic
church, which gained dominance with the adoption of Christianity by the Roman emperors in the fourth century and with
the rise of the papacy and its malign influence on the Christian faith. From the fifth to the sixteenth century thick darkness covered western Christendom. These thousand years
preceding the sixteenth century saw the Catholic clergy and
scholastics combine to destroy classical learning and primitive Christianity by propagating false doctrine and ignorance.
As argued by Théodore Bèze in his *Ecclesiastical History*
(1580), typical Protestant interpretation was that barbarism
and confusion existed in the post-Patristic period. Primitive
faith was reborn and true learning refound only with the
Reformation.

Although disagreeing on the role of Christianity in the decline of the ancient world, humanists and Protestant historians alike saw its end in the fifth century followed by a thousand years of ignorance and barren achievement. They granted that one historical age had been superseded by another and it, by still another—their own. Sixteenth-century men were beginning to see history as a drama in three historical acts—ancient, medieval, and modern. The middle period, the much despised Dark Ages, was increasingly called a *media tempora*. Although this tripartite concept only became current in the sixteenth century, previous writers had spoken of a middle period of history. In 1469 Giovanni Andrea, bishop of Alena, had used the expression *media tempestas*. In 1518 the Swiss scholar Vadian (Joachim von Watt) talked of a *media aetas* while other scholars mentioned *media antiquitas* and *media tempora*. Finally, in 1604 the German legal historian Goldast used the expression *medium aevum*—the Middle Ages—which became an accepted part of historical terminology and thinking with the publication by Cellarius in 1675 of the *Nucleus of Middle History between Ancient and Modern*. This tripartite division of history into ancient, medieval, and modern, a chronological device, has since been used by all historians.

THE ENLIGHTENMENT

Throughout the seventeenth century the humanist interpretation of the ancient world and the Middle Ages prevailed even with historians and philologists such as Charles Du Cange and Jean Mabillon, whose tremendous labors on the Middle Ages were ultimately to provide the foundation for modern research on that period. Interested mainly in compiling dictionaries of medieval Latin or in advancing the techniques of Latin paleography and diplomatic, these *érudits* ignored historical interpretation with the result that their work appeared to provide scholars and *philosophes* of the eighteenth century with further ammunition for a renewed barrage against the Middle Ages. Armed with medieval dictionaries and the editions of medieval writers, eighteenth-century men delighted in comparing the elegant, perfect

Latin of the classical world with the barbarous Latin of the Middle Ages.

In the eighteenth century the writing of history became extremely popular, more comprehensive and synthetic, and more philosophical. Most sympathetic to the ideas of the Renaissance humanists, eighteenth-century men accepted the guidelines of both humanists and Protestant historians regarding the ancient world and the Middle Ages. Fusing a high level of literary style with rational thought, searching for general and broad historical causes, imbued with optimistic ideas of progress, and convinced as were Renaissance men that history should be didactic, historians and philosophers of the Enlightenment accepted the principal ideas of Renaissance historiography and filtered them through their rational and progressive perspective. They praised the brilliant cultural advance of the ancient world, bitterly decried the medieval barbarism and superstition destructive of Graeco-Roman achievements, and thanked Renaissance humanists for stopping this ghastly historical age and placing history again on the road toward progress which, they were convinced, they would greatly accelerate through reason. Like the humanists, they despised medieval Latin letters, Gothic art, and scholasticism. Like the Protestant historians, they lashed out at the medieval church which to them was the archetype of irrationality, ignorance, and superstition. Appalled by what they thought they saw in the Middle Ages, they condemned all that was medieval because, if medieval, it was stupid. Lettered men of the eighteenth century vied with each other in ridiculing the Middle Ages. In an *Essay on the Manners and the Spirit of Nations* (1756) Voltaire (1694–1778), in discussing civilization from Charlemagne to Louis XIII of France, heaped satire upon a barbarous age. Convinced by the humanists that the German barbarism had destroyed a great civilization, he proclaimed that it was necessary "to know the history of that age [Middle Ages] only in order to scorn it," that even in the late fifteenth century "barbarism, superstition, ignorance covered the face of the world, except in Italy." [8] If he believed in a kind of law of historical progress

8. Voltaire, *Essai sur les moeurs et l'esprit des nations, et sur les principaux faits de l'histoire, depuis Charlemagne jusqu'à Louis XIII,* in *Oeuvres complètes,* XII, 123. For an English translation of this work see Voltaire, *Works* (New York, 1901).

well illustrated in his opinion by the Renaissance and his own age, he also seems to have attributed a rhythm to historical progress with civilization undergoing cycles of rise and decline. In his *Dictionnaire philosophique* (1764) he categorically asserted that the Roman Empire "fell because it existed, for it is after all a fact that everything must fall." In his view of the Middle Ages, Condorcet differed with Voltaire only in crediting the Crusades, through the contact they produced between the West and Moslem culture, with lifting the veil of ignorance that had darkened Christian Europe since its inundation by the barbarians.

English rationalists such as Henry Bolingbroke (1678–1751) and David Hume (1711–1776), concurring with their French colleagues, mostly ignored the Middle Ages and concentrated upon important European cultural developments since the Renaissance. One lone historian, William Robertson, discussed the Middle Ages, and he did so in his history of Europe from the end of the Roman Empire to the early sixteenth century (1769) simply to compare the progress of Europe since the Renaissance with the medieval "confusion and barbarism." Historical writing in Germany and Italy overwhelmingly mirrored that in France and England. Only Girolamo Tiraboschi (1731–1794), the learned librarian of Modena, regarded the Middle Ages with other than ridicule. While accepting the traditional explanation for the decline of the Roman Empire and the disastrous consequences, he perceived a slight improvement in culture under Charlemagne and a decided revival in the late twelfth century that led to the dramatic Renaissance of the fourteenth and fifteenth centuries. Such praise for the Middle Ages, though faint, was indeed rare in the eighteenth century when historians were certain that their reasonable and sophisticated tomes had conclusively established the validity of the humanist-Protestant historical interpretation of the catastrophe that befell the ancient world.

Psychologically in accord with the humanists, Montesquieu (1689-1755) and Gibbon, the only scholars to concentrate seriously upon the decline and fall of the Roman Empire as a historical problem and to study its consequences for the subsequent history of western Europe, did not essentially revise the humanist explanation. Convinced that history should be used as a reservoir for the discovery of the "laws of history" and curious as a loyal member of the French nobility about the origins of his class and its role in history, Montesquieu turned back to the Middle Ages to see how the French nobility acquired power. Discovering that it had come through feudalism, he investigated early Germanic institutions which, he believed, had fathered vassalage and other elements of the feudal system. This led him to ask how it happened that the German tribes occupied the western part of the empire and to suggest some answers in *Considerations on the Causes of the Greatness of the Romans and their Decline* (1743). Although an enthusiastic admirer of Roman republican institutions, he argued that republican conquests were at the root of the decline. He wrote in Chapter IX entitled "Two Causes of Rome's Decline" that when Rome expanded outside Italy, distant and long campaigns produced a loss of civic spirit and loyalty among the legions and made the generals too powerful for the Roman Senate to control. The result was civil war, Julius Caesar, and the empire. Conquest also put under Roman rule too many people who lacked the Roman virtues and who, when granted citizenship, did not possess the ability or will to preserve the state. Contributing to the decline were the division and hostility among classes, increasing differences in poverty and wealth exacerbating social tension and causing civil war, the degeneration of morals, and the loss of belief in the old gods. Due to this moral and political decay the republic succumbed to the empire which, resting upon tyranny, inevitably disintegrated. Imperial decline, not too serious until the last of the Antonine emperors in A.D. 180, became disastrous during the civil wars of the third century. Disunited and weakened, the empire was easy prey to the many German tribes that pushed simultaneously over the borders. "It was not," wrote Montesquieu, "a particular invasion that destroyed the empire, but all of them together. . . . But it [the empire] went by slow degrees from decline to fall, until it suddenly collapsed under Arcadius and Honorius [A.D. 400]." [9] Correlating Germans with barbarians, Montesquieu considered them the decisive cause for Rome's catastrophic end. Hobbled for centuries to come, western Europe suffered still

9. Montesquieu, *Considerations on the Causes of the Greatness of the Romans and Their Decline,* p. 178.

further in the early Middle Ages because "the Gothic nations on one side, and the Arabs on the other, had ruined commerce and industry everywhere else." [10]

To sum up and present all that historians had said about the end of the ancient world and to add ideas of his own was the aim of Gibbon in his monumental study. If only for its beautifully expressive prose, Gibbon's history would have become a classic, but in addition it dwarfed previous works on the subject in the depth of its research. Accepting the ideas of the *philosophes* and therefore imbued with admiration for the classical world and revulsion for the Middle Ages, Gibbon, though not objective, was armed with an extraordinary knowledge of the sources available. Unlike Voltaire and Montesquieu, who merely dipped into them to confirm their preconceived notions, he extracted everything possible from them. He ascribed to Christianity a central role for Rome's decline, not because it lost its primitive nature, as believed by previous historians, especially the Protestant historians of the Reformation, but because it destroyed reason by substituting belief in the supernatural and by promoting superstition and ignorance.

EDWARD GIBBON

Gibbon, acknowledging in his *Memoirs* that he was stimulated by Montesquieu's "boldness of hypothesis," accepted much of what Montesquieu said and, it must be emphasized, also largely accepted the arguments of the Renaissance and Protestant historians. In the spirit of this historiographical tradition he was unstinting in his criticism of Roman moral corruption, feebleness of purpose, lack of civic responsibility, venality of officials, insatiate desire for wealth and luxury, and drift away from qualities that had characterized the republic and the empire until A.D. 180. In the wake of the Good Emperors (the Antonines) effeminacy, superstition, religiosity, corruption, and degeneracy rose like a mighty flood to submerge Rome's greatness. Like the humanists and the Protestant historians, Gibbon regarded the fourth and fifth

10. *Ibid.*, p. 214.

centuries as the boundary between ancient and medieval. With the deposition of the pitiful boy emperor Romulus Augustulus by the German leader Odoacer in 476, the empire in the West ended and rapidly succumbed to barbarization. In chapters on the late imperial period and notably in the Appendix, "General Observations on the Fall of the Roman Empire in the West," following Chapter XXXVIII, Gibbon stresses the theme that decline and fall were almost bound to occur with an empire so huge and so immoderately great.

Where Gibbon diverged from humanist, Protestant, and eighteenth-century historical writing was in his treatment of Constantine. He saw the fourth century as he saw his own, an age when civilization changed in direction, and he saw the reign of Constantine (306–337) as a microcosm of Rome's decline and fall which heralded the end of classical civilization in the West and the advent of a long, dark night of ignorance and superstition—the Middle Ages. He masterfully portrays the reign of Constantine as a study in decay and degeneracy when an ambitious, talented, ruthless, and cynical man used the Christian faith to further his political designs. For the first time emerges the interpretation that Constantine, seeing in Christianity the religion of the future, a religion that expressed the collective tendencies of the age, embraced it only to buttress his power and to unify the empire. Observing paganism in decay everywhere around him, he favored Christianity because it emphasized obedience. Thinking the Christian faith would be good insurance for his enormous crimes and sins, he was baptized just before dying. Cynical and calculating to the end, Constantine never believed, only used. But his tactics enabled Christianity, the chief enemy of the empire, to strangle and destroy it. This interpretation of Constantine, seasoned with eighteenth-century thought and bias, now stood beside the other traditional explanations. In *The Age of Constantine*, Jacob Burckhardt (1818–1897) acknowledged his debt to Gibbon in writing that a man such as Constantine "is essentially unreligious, even if he pictures himself standing in the midst of a churchly community." [11] While one may disagree with Thomas Carlyle (1795–1881) who wrote that Gibbon, by basing his interpretation of the decline and fall of the Roman Empire on "Christianity and

11. Burckhardt, *The Age of Constantine*, p. 280.

Barbarism," constructed a beautiful bridge joining the ancient and the modern worlds, one cannot deny that Gibbon's famous interpretation is still preeminent in the historiography concerned with this classic problem.

All that had been said before on the end of the ancient world and the beginning of the Middle Ages, Gibbon first restated or reinterpreted with eighteenth-century perspective and vocabulary, then added his rationalist interpretation of Christianity. Combined and synthesized in his exquisite prose, his thought became a monument of historiography dominating historical writing in the nineteenth century. What is remarkable about Gibbon's interpretation is that so little of it was altered or questioned in the nineteenth century, that century of *Historismus* which fostered so many new trends and improvements in historical research arising from the "scientific" methodology and from such European movements as romanticism, nationalism, and liberalism, but few new explanations for the end of the ancient world. Historians mostly refined and redefined the traditional explanations. In the grip of specialization that characterized nineteenth-century historiography, classical historians unquestioningly accepted the fifth century as the termination for ancient history and concentrated their research before this century, while medievalists, finally coming into their own, were content to begin their histories of the Middle Ages with a description of how the Germans had destroyed the empire during the fourth and fifth centuries.

2. From Gibbon to Pirenne

THE MIDDLE AGES REHABILITATED

For medievalists the major historical development of the nineteenth century was the rehabilitation of the Middle Ages as an age demanding sympathetic study and understanding if men hoped to unearth their cultural, spiritual, and institutional heritage and, above all, to trace the birth of their own nations. Initially, little of value sprang from the enthusiasm engendered by the romantic reaction against eighteenth-century classicism and reason. Much said stemmed from sentiment rather than from new knowledge of the Middle Ages, but this romantic spirit was psychologically important because it ended the defensive mentality of medievalists and inspired them to take the offensive. Idealizing the Middle Ages, the romantics praised what previous historians had disdained. They admired Gothic art, ceased to equate the medieval church with superstition and ignorance, glorified the Middle Ages as the Age of Faith, disassociated feudalism from anarchy, and began to extol the various vernacular literatures. In tune with the rising tide of nationalism, they stressed that national origins were rooted in the Middle Ages; that the unique characteristics of the French, Germans, Italians, and English were formed in the Middle Ages; and that their respective racial qualities explained superior cultural achievement and national greatness.

The search for national origins in the Middle Ages was fueled by the new racial doctrines of Count Joseph Arthur de Gobineau and Houston Stewart Chamberlain. In a treatise

Essai sur l'inégalité des races humaines (1854) Gobineau proclaimed the complete superiority of the Aryan or Teutonic race whose members, he was convinced, started western European civilization. Patrician by birth, an ardent royalist, and a conservative Catholic, Gobineau, like Montesquieu, searched for the origin of the French aristocracy and found it in the Franks whom he regarded as members of the Teutonic master race. He naturally idealized the Middle Ages, when a feudal aristocracy held the political power and dominated society. Chamberlain concurred with Gobineau, arguing in *Foundations of the Nineteenth Century* (1899) that the Middle Ages were decisive because in that period came "the awakening of the Teutonic peoples to the consciousness of their all-important vocation as the founders of a completely new civilization and culture." [12] In one stroke he exonerated the Germans from the charge that they were the culprits responsible for one thousand years of barbarism and credited their genius with the founding of European civilization and even with making possible the Renaissance.

Such encouragement, however fallacious, sent eager medievalists to probing the available evidence. Except for a few who completely adopted the racist ideas of Gobineau and Chamberlain, they concluded that the Germans deserved serious study and that the early Middle Ages, when the Germans put down their roots across western Europe, needed greater illumination. Agreeing with classical historians that the period before the fifth century was ancient and that what followed was medieval, they concentrated on studying the early Germans and their influence upon European civilization. In their evaluations, nationalism was a potent force. English and German medievalists were much more sympathetic to early Germanic achievements than were the French and Italian. Historians who praised the Germans were said to belong to the Germanist school and those unsympathetic to the Germans, to the Romanist school. During the second half of the nineteenth century these schools debated the origins and significance of such medieval institutions as seignorial-

12. Chamberlain, *Die Grundlagen des neunzehnten Jahrhunderts,* I, 6. For the English translation see John Lees, *Foundations of the Nineteenth Century, by Houston Stewart Chamberlain* (New York, 1914), 2 vols.

ism, feudalism, and the town. Germanists argued that the
servile seignorial system stemmed from a late Roman imperial
agrarian system that gradually imposed itself upon the free
Germans who had previously lived in democratically or com-
munally free agrarian villages known as the *Markgenossen-
schaft*. The Romanists denied that the Germans had ever lived
in such agrarian communities, convinced instead that they
had lived under an agrarian system similar to that of the late
imperial period. With feudalism, the debate centered upon
whether it was an anarchical, decentralist, and destructive
political and military system or whether it had constructive
features. Those who considered it chaotic argued that it was
Germanic in origin. Germanists countered by attempting to
derive it from late imperial institutions or to prove that it was
actually a resourceful and constructive political system. Such
debate raged even into the period following World War I.

Despite the rehabilitation of the Middle Ages, the stimulating debates, and the magnificent scholarship of the medievalists, little of the Gibbonesque interpretation changed
during the nineteenth and early part of the twentieth century.
Classical and medieval historians continued to regard each
other across the no-man's-land that was the fifth century, a
kind of iron curtain that separated ancient from medieval.
Medievalists rarely concerned themselves with the decline of
the Roman Empire in the West, preferring to leave this
problem to classical historians. Instead, they indulged in
painstaking research, characteristic of the universally admired method of Leopold von Ranke, in an attempt to do for
the Middle Ages what had been done so long by classical
historians for Greek and Roman history. Only after World
War I did medievalists begin to ask when, how, and why the
ancient world gave way to the medieval.

From the debates of historians during the nineteenth and
early part of the twentieth century it is obvious that, while
working within the framework of Gibbon, historians at-
tempted to buttress or modify his interpretation through their
increased knowledge of classical sources and appreciation of
the value of epigraphy, archaeology, art history, economics,
sociology, psychology, and the biological sciences. In defining
progress and decadence, in seeking the symptoms and roots
of decay in a society, and in probing possible means to reverse

or arrest the decline of a civilization, they wrote, essentially, a chapter in nineteenth and early twentieth-century historiography.

RELIGIOUS AND MYSTICAL THEORIES

In contrast to humanist thinkers and historians of the Enlightenment who had generally assigned Rome's decline to political and moral circumstances, to human actions and decisions over which man had some control, some later historians introduced causes largely religious or mystical. Some saw the rise and fall of empires in Christian prophetic terms that rested upon an apocalyptic portrait of the well-known world kingdoms or six world ages. Others interpreted history in a more sophisticated approach with civilizations going through cycles. This cyclical interpretation, propounded first by Plato to account for the frequent change in the forms of government of the Greek city-states—tyrannies, oligarchies, aristocracies, democracies, and ochlocracies—was popular with Greek and Roman historians, and especially Polybius (205?– 125 B.C.), whose ideas were adopted by Machiavelli in the sixteenth century and by Vico in the eighteenth in his search for universal laws of history. Evidence for the cyclical theory is not convincing, either for the age of the Greek city-state or that of the Renaissance. No historian has been able to prove that any Greek or Italian city-state passed through any of the model cycles.

Akin to the cyclical explanation is the biological, predominant in nineteenth-century historical writing, that regarded history as a series of civilizations, each reproducing the growth and decline of a living organism in accordance with biological laws. How often historians have used the phrase "law of decay" as though they had established a scientific law accounting for the decay of states and civilizations. Gobineau repeatedly compared human society to living organisms, contending that each society or state has among its elements of life the principle of inevitable death. The most notable attempt to equate civilizations to organisms with life cycles was that of the German philosopher Oswald Spengler (1880–1936) who predicted the eclipse of western civilization in a massive work, *Decline of the West: An Outline of a Morphology of World History,* that is sprinkled with such statements as "Cultures are organisms, and world-history is their collective biography. . . . Every culture passes through the age-phases of the individual man. Each has its childhood, youth, manhood, and old age. . . . The duration of a generation—whatever may be its nature—is a fact of almost mystical significance."[13] Spengler argued that classical civilization's fundamental imprint was the Greek concept of man. For the Greeks, to exist was to be corporeal; reality always took a physical form. When classical civilization decayed and died it was succeeded by a magical civilization, that of the Christians and Arabs, whose history was a struggle between body and soul, good and evil. What Spengler identified as western or Faustian civilization began to emerge about 1000. Such history, though stimulating, lacks the evidence requisite for the validity of historical interpretations and conclusions. As with the cyclical theory, there is no evidence that there is a morphology of history, that civilizations, like animals and plants, come into being, live, and die. Spengler's approach to history is neither historical nor philosophical, but mystical.

Not wholly in sympathy with Spengler, Arnold Toynbee was however intrigued by some of his ideas. The theme that societies and civilizations are not determined by natural laws but by human actions and decisions prevails throughout the twelve volumes of Toynbee's *Study of History* (1934–1961). Man appears constantly presented with challenges from his natural environment and from the historical events of his life span, and his response to these challenges determines the structural growth of his society. When his response is positive, his civilization flourishes; when negative, it withers and dies. According to Toynbee, Greek classical civilization failed and was destroyed by war because of its inability to establish an international community. Rome forged such a community but erred in basing it on force, thereby undermining authority. Toynbee ascribes the fall of Rome to internal and external opposition. The opposition to authority within came from the masses who turned away from the state to higher values, to new gods, to oriental mystery religions and Christianity, while

13. Spengler, *The Decline of the West,* pp. 104–113.

from without came the pressure of the Germans. Under these onslaughts Roman society collapsed and there emerged Christianity and a new civilization—the medieval. In generalizing that civilizations rise and fall upon the quality of their response to environmental and human challenges, Toynbee, like Spengler, has constructed a theory unsupported by the evidence. His interpretation is only slightly less mystical than Spengler's.

THE ELEMENT OF RACE

To dismiss these pseudo-scientific and mystical explanations without further elaboration is possible, but attempts to connect the failure of Rome to race must be considered seriously, particularly when they purport to have applied Darwinism to history. Darwinism so applied leads to the conclusions that civilizations based upon the fittest men survive and thrive while those based upon the unfit fail and die, that civilizations where the fittest decrease and become outnumbered by the unfit decay and wither away, and that the fit become weakened when they marry the less fit. Any analysis of these efforts discloses how unscientific and unjustified it is to apply Darwin's law of natural selection to history. It cannot be proved that certain races are definitely superior to others, that some and not others are capable of creating and preserving a great civilization. Even the most scholarly of these attempts have been conceived from bias and prejudice or from nationalistic devotion and are rooted in racial discrimination. Witness the malevolent theories of Gobineau and Chamberlain!

In perhaps the most patent attempt to establish race as the cause for the fall of the Roman Empire, M. P. Nilsson has argued in *Imperial Rome* (1926) that the quality of Roman civilization depended upon racial character and that alien races and barbarian tribes, to be assimilated, must be interpenetrated by the conquered. Unfortunately, because the Romans did not succeed in interpenetrating those who conquered them, their birthrate declined while that of the non-Romans increased, Roman blood was diluted by inter-

marriage, and the mingling of races produced not Romanization but a mongrelization that spread across the empire,
resulting in the loss of stable spiritual and moral standards
and the death of a proud civilization. The rebuttal to this
interpretation of the Romans as a kind of master race is that
they simply appropriated the rich cultures that the conquered
Greeks and peoples of the Middle East had already created.
Who can say that Roman ability to build roads and a rational
system of law is superior to Greek literary, artistic, and philosophical talent or to eastern religious perception? Why also
did the eastern Roman Empire, the Byzantine, that was
essentially Greek and eastern, survive a thousand years after
the Roman Empire in the West was no longer a political
entity?

In a more recent attempt to apply race to historical causation Tenney Frank (1876–1939) has studied 13,900 sepulchral
inscriptions and has concluded that Rome and the Latin West
were inundated by Greek and oriental slaves who, as they
became emancipated and achieved citizenship, changed the
character of the Latin West. He has estimated that, ultimately,
ninety percent of Rome's inhabitants were of foreign origin
and that "this orientalizing of Rome's populace has a more
important bearing than is usually accorded it upon the larger
question of why the spirit and acts of imperial Rome are
totally different from those of the republic," a situation that
inevitably created the triumph of oriental despotism or abso-
lutism, the popularity of oriental mystery religions, the decline
in the quality of Latin literature, and the disappearance of
those Romans with a flair for government who had built the
empire. Rome's disintegration is explained by "the fact that
the people who built Rome had given away to a different
race."[14] Frank is as racist in his arguments as Nilsson. Further
epigraphical research has also placed in doubt Frank's statis-
tics, suggesting that his sample is invalid and that he has
confused eastern with western slaves.

A more subtle racist interpretation is that of Otto Seeck
who, in his well-known book on the decline of the ancient
world (1901), has saddled the emperors of the third century
with the responsibility for Rome's troubles. He accuses them

14. Frank, "Race Mixture in the Roman Empire," *American Historical Review,* XXI (1916), 705.

of constant *Ausrottung der Besten* (extermination of the best) by consciously eliminating capacity and individual merit until an atmosphere developed that abhorred accomplishment and quality and that encouraged a slave mentality whose logical result was the triumph of Christianity which he calls *die Religion des Betteltums* (the beggars' religion). Originality disappeared but, even worse, men retained no faith in their own ability, courage, or reason; they surrendered their reason to faith and their fate to the all-powerful emperor. While Seeck cannot be accused of Nilsson's racism because he does not attribute the degeneration of character and ability to racial inferiority or mongrelization, he still embraces a kind of inverted Darwinism that accounts for the disappearance of originality, courage, and reason. His argument is vitiated by a deep and lifelong hatred of Christianity which, in a sense simply repeating Gibbon's famous remarks about it, he indicts for its patience, pusillanimity, discouragement of active civic virtues, and the destruction of military spirit. Difficult to understand is how Seeck can categorize men of the fourth and fifth centuries as deficient in courage and ability when Ferdinand Lot has justifiably ranked some of the late emperors far above the Julio-Claudians and others, calling them "supermen." Who is prepared to write off a Diocletian or a Constantine and his accomplishments won in the face of overwhelming odds? Who can accept lumping men such as St. Ambrose and St. Augustine among the cowardly and fawning puppets of the emperors? Above all, how can Seeck justify his theory of the hereditary transmissibility of virtue?

Related to these racial interpretations are those which argue that the aristocratic, governing classes of the republic declined disastrously in the centuries just before and after Christ and that the majority suffered extinction, a loss disastrous for the empire because it meant the extinction of those with political ability and military prowess. Even if some of the aristocracy became soft because of their wealth and leisure and even if some indulged in physical vice, such practice was not widespread enough to result in severe diminution of numbers or of the capacity to govern and fight. While there is some evidence to support the conclusion that aristocratic families did not reproduce as abundantly as the lower social classes, failing often even to reproduce or to marry, a tendency

that so concerned Augustus he enacted legislation to coun-
teract it, and that such a trend may have extinguished some
highly gifted families in Rome itself, this does not seem to
have happened to comparable families in the provinces. Too
frequently historians have generalized only from what they
know about Rome, a practice which is no more valid than
generalizing about Great Britain, France, and the United
States from evidence pertinent only to London, Paris, and
New York City. Tacitus (*ca.* 55–117), the Roman historian of
the first century who violently detested emperorship and who
castigated the aristocratic classes for having surrendered
their political power to Augustus and the Julio-Claudians,
attributed some of the aristocratic woes to high living, soft-
ness, and effete habits, and unfavorably compared the Roman
aristocracy to the Germans who, in his eyes, exemplified courage, industry, and family fidelity. But, it must be emphasized,
Tacitus was only generalizing from what he observed in
Rome and, despite his literary talent, wrote biased history in-
tended to discredit the political system of the empire. That
homosexuality weakened the manly fiber of the Romans and
blunted their political and creative capacity has been asserted
but not proven. Homosexuality there was, but less than in
Athens which produced a brilliant culture and, in any event,
has it been demonstrated that homosexuals have less capacity
than others?

POPULATION DECLINE

No historian can deny that a gradual or sharp decline in population is an unhealthy development that can have
ruinous effects on the economy and, if unchecked, can place
a civilization in jeopardy. Neighbors with greater manpower
may be tempted to conquer a state demographically inferior.
From Napoleon's time almost to the present the population of
France has declined or remained stable for long periods with
the result that France, slim in manpower, has barely survived
military and economic crises during the nineteenth and twentieth centuries. Could it be possible that a decline in population caused the Roman Empire to fall? Historians have often

contended that disease and epidemics resulted in catastrophe. Some have argued that the Great Plague which swept across the empire in A.D. 167 decimated the population. Granted that for the short term such population loss must have been serious, it could not have been important over a long term because demographers have shown that populations bounce back quickly after disease and plague. Likewise, economic historians have proved that economic conditions rapidly normalize themselves. It is now accepted, for example, that the Black Death which devastated Europe between 1348 and 1350 had only short-term consequences and was not a catastrophe which changed the course of European history. Also, historians now realize that those who have seen malaria as endemic throughout the Mediterranean world have generalized almost solely upon evidence taken from the shores of Latium and Etruria where indeed it was. Doctors and epidemologists have shown, however, that the Mediterranean climate and land structure have never favored the stagnant waters and swamps essential for the mosquito to thrive. Recently some historians of science and medicine have suggested that lead poisoning took a great toll among the Romans because they used lead pipes for laying on their water and for some of their cooking. The rebuttal of scientists is that no deleterious reaction comes from lead water pipes and that only certain foods are affected adversely when cooked in lead utensils.

Rather than ascribing population decline in the Roman Empire solely to disease or to race suicide among the aristocratic classes, A. E. R. Boak (1888–1962) has ascribed it to a combination of natural and human causes. Detecting first a decline in the rural population which cultivated lands for the urban inhabitants, he then saw by the third century a serious decline in the urban population. Arguing that once the birthrate of a people begins to decline it does so in a geometrical rather than an arithmetical ratio, he concluded that the third century witnessed a catastrophic decline in population which he linked to epidemics, the anarchy of the empire between 235 and 284, wars, starvation, and forcible deportation of large segments of the people. The population then decreased until the empire expired in the West and continued this downward movement until the tenth century. Boak saw this population loss resulting in a rural class inade-

quate for cultivating the land; a crushing burden of taxation
upon what land was tilled; destructive taxation of the urban
population, especially the *curiales* (municipal senators); in-
sufficient manpower for the armies necessary to defend the
frontier against the Germans; and lack of personnel for the
government. Emperors like Diocletian and Constantine were
compelled to organize all elements of Roman society into
castes which they forced to perform the political, military, and
economic functions vital for the survival of the state. This
social stratification, conscription, and forced labor undermined
morale and destroyed initiative. Faced with declining manpower and increasing impoverishment, Boak concluded, the
empire was "unable to defend itself against disintegration
from within and invasion from without" and "staggered slowly
on to its inevitable dissolution." [15]

Boak has rightly described the developments in the third
and fourth centuries, but were the consequences as grave as
he thought and, if so, why were they limited to the West while
the empire in the East survived? Even if he had searched, he
could not have produced population figures to prove his argument because they are unobtainable, and without the statis-
tics essential for the demographer it is impossible to measure
population in the ancient world except haphazardly. Even
such careful studies of Rome as those of K. J. Beloch (1854–
1929) and F. Lot (1866–1952) are based upon questionable
techniques. It is obvious that whatever figures are obtained
by knowing the area of the city of Rome at a certain date and
allotting so much space to each house for a family of a certain
size are arbitrary and inexact.

CLIMATIC CHANGE AND SOIL EXHAUSTION

Economists and geographers have assigned the
principal role in destroying the Roman Empire to climatic
change and exhaustion of the soil and minerals. In a series of
studies during the first quarter of the twentieth century the
American geographer Ellsworth Huntington (1876–1947)

15. Boak, *Manpower Shortage and the Fall of the Roman Empire in
the West*, p. 129.

tried to relate the growth pattern of the great sequoias of California to the troubles of the Roman Empire in the fourth and fifth centuries. Arguing that the climates of California and the Mediterranean world are similar and have always undergone the same climatic modifications, he charted the growth of the sequoias and concluded that during the fourth and fifth centuries there was in California and therefore also in the Mediterranean world a hot and dry climate. So serious was this climate for agriculture and other economic occupations that the empire died. This theory, however intriguing, has difficulties. When Huntington conducted his research there were records of California rainfall only for the previous fifty years and none for the ancient world, a situation making any comparison dangerous. Furthermore, some geographers have questioned his assumption that the California and Mediterranean climates are so alike, and some historians, including Michael Rostovtzeff, have produced evidence that the fourth and fifth centuries were not hot and dry.

But what of soil exhaustion? Was it so serious that it struck a fatal blow at agriculture making the sustenance of a large population impossible? The answer is yes according to some agronomists, economists, and economic historians. From study of Italian soil and ancient agriculture J. Liebig (1803–1873) and V. G. Simkhovitch (1874–1959) have found evidence that lands were denuded of forests and trees and became exhausted from serious erosion, improper drainage of the soil, inadequate fertilization, and failure to practice crop rotation; all of which led to deserted farms, barren soil, swampy land, and a general flight from the land. There is no doubt that some of this occurred but how general was it? Too much of the evidence comes from Italy or Sicily without acknowledgement that the valley of the Nile was annually renourished or that such areas as Gaul with a different climate and soil were not affected. It is true that various Roman authors refer to lands that went from farming to grazing and then became deserted. It is also true that the lands ringing the Mediterranean require more irrigation and more attention than those to the north. From the first-century writer Columella we learn that crop rotation, the planting of leguminous plants, and marling were applied to improve crop yields. Was, then, soil exhaustion so serious as to account for the failure of the empire in the West? And if so, what sustained the empire in the East where so much of the land was equally arid and required intensive irrigation and care? If Rome secured the bulk of her grain from the Nile Valley during the first and second centuries, why could she not continue to do so in the centuries following? When farmers fled to the cities leaving deserted lands behind them was it not because of the intolerable taxation in kind instituted by Diocletian? When Constantine decreed in 330 that all the peasant cultivators (*coloni*) must remain on the land and that their condition would henceforth be heritable, he did so because the land had to be cultivated to produce the necessary food and taxes. If it had been so exhausted and incapable of producing food and other essential products, it seems unlikely that he would have taken this drastic step, the first leading toward the seignorial system under which the peasant was bound to the soil of the large estate. These objections receive support from an interesting experiment by the German agronomist T. H. von Thünen (1783–1850) who, over a long term, duplicated as closely as possible ancient agrarian routine and techniques on soil comparable to that of imperial Italy. His results led him to declare that the fertility of the soil remained unimpaired so long as an adequate number of cattle was kept and the amount of pasture was properly adjusted to that of arable crops. He also argued that absolute exhaustion seemed to be impossible and that the failure to add phosphorus in proportion to the phosphorus removed is much less serious than Liebig thought, as long as the condition of the soil is well maintained. It is, he contends, misleading to describe land as "exhausted" when for a period arable crops cannot be profitably grown. Such a period may be short and crops may again be profitably planted. Obviously Roman agriculture did not employ modern farming techniques and some mineral depletion occurred, but its effect upon agriculture cannot have been as serious as supposed. Since there are no soil analyses for the imperial period and the question can never be definitively resolved, it seems reasonable to conclude that lands became uncultivated and deserted in the fourth and fifth centuries because of misgovernment, crushing taxation, and lack of incentive. Even in Egypt at this time lands were deserted and irrigation systems allowed to disintegrate, and certainly not because of soil exhaustion!

POLITICAL AND MILITARY IMPACT

Historians intrigued by political causation have not advanced the argument much beyond that of the Renaissance humanists. An interpretation favored by classical historians is that the failure of the Roman Republic caused the loss of political liberty and civic devotion which then led to imperial autocracy resting upon military force. During the last years of the republic when a very narrow aristocratic class with a monopoly over political power neglected its responsibility to maintain political order and to redress social and economic ills, its power went to such aspiring generals as Marius, Sulla, Pompey, Caesar, and finally to Augustus. The concentration of all power in the emperor, so the argument runs, destroyed the qualities of self-help and resourcefulness characteristic of the city-state and earlier republican history. It is true that the advent of the empire had some psychological effect but that it destroyed an essential *esprit* is dubious. By the first century B.C. the republic had reached a dead end. It could no longer govern or solve the problems created by acquiring a Mediterranean empire. Without the imperial solution of Augustus, chaos and disintegration might have come in the first century B.C. As it turned out, the empire solved many of the problems of the republic and provided a viable political structure for almost another four hundred years. Most emperors, it must be noted, were conscientious, industrious, and able, and under them the provinces were better administered than under the aristocratic senate of the republic. The inhabitants of the city-state, therefore, had more reason to be loyal to the emperors than to the senate. That they flagged in civic devotion or effort is neither evident nor proven until late in the political life of the empire.

A fatal weakness of imperial rule in the eyes of some historians was lack of hereditary succession to the emperorship which provoked disputed successions and civil wars, with the legions assuming the role of kingmaker. While friction did occur at various periods, especially in the third century, it must be balanced against the political stability of the Julio-Claudian period or that of the Antonines when there was likewise no principle of heritability. In the Hellenistic monarchies succession was heritable, but this did not preserve them. Guglielmo Ferrero (1871–1942) has, in fact, dealt severely with Marcus Aurelius because he arranged for his incompetent son Commodus to succeed him rather than consulting the senate and designating the ablest man as his successor. When Commodus was assassinated the emperorship was then determined by the will of the legions and the result was Septimius Severus (193–211) who openly admitted that his power rested upon military strength. Thereafter the senate had no power and there arose what Ferrero has termed a crisis in political authority. Henceforth the emperorship was determined by war and revolution, a development that destroyed the empire. Ferrero believed that the monarchical system succeeded in the East because there it was rooted in the traditions, practices, and emotions. But in the West the monarchical principle had no tradition or support. According to Ferrero, "the principle of authority is the key to all civilization; when the political system becomes disintegrated and falls into anarchy, civilization in its turn is rapidly broken up." [16]

But why does a civilization fail to develop a political system that will sustain it? Seeking an answer in the history of British political experience during the nineteenth and twentieth centuries, W. E. Heitland (1847–1935) attributed Roman political failure to the inability to ascertain "the will of the actual majority of citizens," to develop political institutions whereby programs are submitted to electorates who in turn "delegate the function of final judgment to representatives," or to learn the delegation of responsibility.[17] What he considered lacking in the Roman political system was English parliamentary government as it developed after the Reform Act of 1832. To ask for or to expect such government to develop in the ancient world is unrealistic. Not even during the age of Pericles did Athens approximate parliamentary democracy. Nor have many modern European nations achieved the British success.

16. Ferrero, *The Ruin of Ancient Civilization and the Triumph of Christianity*, p. 207.
17. Heitland, *The Roman Fate*, p. 41.

Another favorite argument of some historians is that Rome could not defend herself militarily against the Germans during the fourth and fifth centuries. Perhaps, the argument runs, the trouble began in the second century B.C. when the republic moving into the eastern Mediterranean became overextended. The frontier may have held firm had the legions, as in the days of the republic and early empire, been composed only of Roman citizens, courageous and devoted to Rome's proud military tradition. But the ranks of the legions had been gradually filled with Germans from the other side of the frontier, and how could such soldiers be expected to equal the military prowess and spirit of the old legionaries when they had not shared in Roman tradition and culture? Another suggestion is that when the legions became professionalized during the first century B.C. they lost their devotion to Rome and thereafter looked to their generals for good pay and advancement, fighting for the general who most satisfactorily rewarded them against any enemy, even the senate or the emperor. Others believe that had Trajan not expanded the frontier eastward from Syria and northeast from the Danube River, Roman forces could have defended the strategically placed *castra* and *castella*. As it was, their strength could not cope with the added burden. E. Kornemann (1868–1946) contends that Augustus reduced the strength of the legions too severely, thereby permanently weakening the military establishment. While there is some evidence for all these suggestions, it is obvious that none of the military developments or strategic decisions were so pervasive that they could not be reversed. Also, let us remember that many of the Germans fought loyally and efficiently for the empire in the fourth and fifth centuries and that the emperors Aurelian, Diocletian, and Constantine had no trouble defending the frontier when they put their minds to it. What is certain is that from the first century B.C. the legions had too much power in the making and unmaking of generals and emperors, a situation inevitably contributing to the breakdown of orderly government as a prelude to civil war and anarchy during the third and fourth centuries. Although individually or collectively these military developments and decisions sapped the health of the empire by creating a feeling of instability, fear, and uncertainty

among the citizens, they alone did not cause the death of a
great civilization.

It has been said that poor administration alienated the
people, led to a loss of faith in those governing, and contributed to undermining the economy, society, and government.
Undeniably progressive depreciation of the coinage and intolerable and arbitrary taxation so weakened the economy
that even Diocletian's Draconian reforms were inadequate.
These stark social and economic measures of Diocletian have
been interpreted by Boak as a desperate means to extract as
large a revenue as possible from the population with the unfortunate result of increasing "departmentalization of the
bureaucracy" and of leading to an "increase in the number of
civil service employees." [18] Swiftly there mushroomed a top-
heavy bureaucracy staffed by non-producers living off the
labors of the diminishing producers. The tax burden inevitably
became higher and exacerbated the economic woes of the
empire. In essence this has also been the argument of A. H. M.
Jones in his massive social, economic, and administrative
history of the late empire (1964), but in addition he has
leveled the charge of corruption and lack of public spirit
against the late imperial bureaucracy. These explanations,
however, do not penetrate very deeply into the imperial trouble. Like a fever, they indicate the presence of a sickness but
not its cause.

INTELLECTUAL AND CULTURAL INFLUENCE

Students of intellectual and cultural history have
criticized Roman education because only the elite were educated. Eventually, with the educated elite outnumbered and
absorbed by the illiterate masses who had no knowledge for
governing or staffing the organs of administration, the empire
ran amuck. This interpretation has been elegantly advanced
by L. Homo in his work on Roman civilization (1930). Also,
although the cutting edge of his argument is economic and
social causation, Rostovtzeff is concerned with the hostility

18. Boak, *Manpower Shortage,* p. 118.

between the educated middle class and the masses who, upon replacing the middle class, lacked the experience and knowledge to make the empire function. No one denies that the mass of the population in the empire was uneducated and had little feeling for Graeco-Roman culture, but has not this been true of the masses in most nations until recently? What is remarkable is that during the first three centuries of the empire education appears to have been more widely diffused than in any subsequent period of western history prior to the nineteenth century. Certainly the profound ignorance of the Roman masses was a serious deficiency that contributed to the demise of classical civilization, but it is unjust to criticize the Roman Empire for not accomplishing what even modern nations find difficult.

While other scholars, less concerned with the distribution of classical education than with its quality, generally agree that the Romans exhibited great skill in their efficient borrowing of Greek culture and showed creativity in their own significant cultural achievements during the last century of the republic and first hundred years of the empire, they detect a decline in literary, philosophical, and artistic creativity thereafter, culminating in fatal degeneration during the third and fourth centuries. Graeco-Roman culture became simply a corpus of knowledge learned and repeated generation after generation, sterile and unrelated to society. In his analysis of Rome's intellectual and artistic sickness in the fifth century, Samuel Dill (1844–1924) portrays intellectuals content to epitomize and interpret previous literature and philosophy and artists satisfied with copying works of their predecessors. This sterility ultimately pervaded every aspect of endeavor, even the crafts, so that when Constantine constructed his triumphal arch in Rome, it had to be modeled upon previous ones and some of the sculptured bas reliefs taken from other arches. As skills degenerated, so too did sense of style and taste. Compared with the art of the golden age, that of the late imperial period was stereotyped and banal.

In the third and fourth centuries intellectuals who still embraced Greek philosophy, particularly that of Stoicism with its emphasis upon reason and natural law, began to repudiate reason and unaided human ability and to turn to the new

Christian faith for comfort and truth, at the same time as the
masses and the middle class were spurning the pagan deities
and embracing the oriental mystery religions in their quest for
nourishment from some mystical supernatural being. Scholars
who equate this intellectual, spiritual, and psychological
change with Rome's degeneration are essentially in accord
with Gibbon. If culture became sterile and inflexible in the
late empire is this not a reflection of a deeper malady? The
artist or intellectual who cannot create has some basic deficiency. But what was basically deficient in the empire at this
time and how does one answer this question when there is so
little evidence affording any basis for measurement? To char-
acterize these centuries of decline as an age of retreat before
reason and as a loss of confidence in human ability falls short
of the mark. Were not the early fathers of the church such as
Jerome, Ambrose, and Augustine more creative and respon-
sive to the needs of society than the sterile, pagan epito-
mizers? Is it possible that classical culture had become so old
and weary that men desperately needed the Christian interpretation of man, his purpose, and his destiny? Sadly, such
speculation, however stimulating, is outside the realm of historians and history.

K. J. Beloch (1854–1929) has suggested that Rome was
fated to perish because she absorbed the Greek city-states
responsible for most of the creative achievements of classical
civilization, which the Romans generally borrowed and
adapted, into a world state and prevented them from fully
developing their creative forces and consolidating the achievements of a promising civilization. But Beloch ignores the facts
of Greek history. In asserting that Rome conquered the Greek
city-states before they had achieved their cultural potential,
he seems to forget that Greek cultural achievement was at its
highest point in the fifth and fourth centuries B.C. even before the age of Alexander the Great. Scientific, mathematical,
and philosophical achievements of the Greeks in the Hellenistic age, however remarkable, were inferior to those preceding. To claim that the Romans cut off Greek creativity by
conquest is therefore erroneous; Greek creative ability had
been waning even before the age of Alexander.

Although armed with abundant evidence on human

thought, motives, and feeling, scholars of modern history still find it extremely difficult to account for transformations in the spirit and mentality of a civilization. In this quest the historian has occasionally used the knowledge of the psychiatrist and social psychologist. Conversely, the psychiatrist has sometimes applied has knowledge to historical evidence, proving new insights into personages and historical periods, as was done for Martin Luther by the psychiatrist Erik Erikson. But the insights of even the most skillful historian or psychiatrist regarding the ancient world are severely limited by the evidence available. Occasionally in modern history there is sufficient evidence to enable historian and psychiatrist to account for the motivations and drives of a man or for the *Weltanschauung* and collective feelings of an age even though the psychiatrist lacks the patient or patients from whom to extract the basic secrets. No one, however, is justified in asserting that he can get inside Pericles, Alexander the Great, Plato, Cicero, or Caesar and account for their drives and accomplishments. One must be satisfied with shrewd speculation, as was Lot while contemplating the reasons for the troubles of the empire. After describing the corruption of public spirit, he stressed the basic transformation in literature, the arts, philosophy, and religion which he ascribed to the oriental mystery religions and Christianity that refocussed man's view toward other values. Men's souls were detached from the "ancient forms of beauty." Art, succumbing to eastern styles, sacrificed line and nobility of character to color, to the fantastic, and to the chimerical. Condemned by the Christian church, pagan literature was no longer understood or loved and the new Christian literature in Greek and Latin, lacking literary form, did not fill the void. Science, philosophy, and reason receded before the tide of oriental mysticism. This transformation, Lot believed, "altered the psychology of the man of antiquity," but the evidence did not allow him to pursue this idea.[19] Lack of evidence still prevents the historian and psychiatrist from probing deeper into a possible psychological alteration of the classical world.

19. Lot, *The End of the Ancient World and the Beginnings of the Middle Ages*, p. 186. Lot wrote (p. 2) that "a break had occurred in psychological continuity."

SOCIAL AND ECONOMIC CAUSATION

At the time of Gibbon, historians had little appreciation of social and economic history. It is precisely in
this field of research that modern historians have contributed the most. Because of the industrialization of Europe in
the nineteenth century, works of Karl Marx (1818–1883) in-
sisting upon economic causation as the explanation of historical development, the pioneer work of Auguste Comte
(1798–1857) in social classes and related problems, and the
basic research of German economic historians such as Gustav
Schmoller, the nineteenth century became aware of the im-
plications of economic and social phenomena. Consequently,
by the late nineteenth century important research was being
done on ancient social and economic history.

One of the first scholars to explain the decline of the ancient
world in terms of economic development was W. L. Westermann (1873–1954). Dismissing Gibbon's barbarism and Christianity, he found as cause for decline the economic system
taken over by Rome when she conquered the East. In the
Hellenistic monarchies of Asia Minor and Africa agriculture
took the form of large estates cultivated by a dependent
peasantry, and when this system was introduced to the West
it ended the small farm worked by the free farmer. Arguing
that the free Roman farmer had been the backbone of Rome's
success, Westermann insisted that his disappearance had serious consequences for the ancient economy and culture. With
the large estate worked first by slaves and then by a dependent
peasantry (the colonate) came a decline in buying power, a
shrinking market for the products of the city, and the imposition
upon the middle governing class (the *curiales*) of tax collecting, an impossible assignment when agricultural resources
dried up. Forced to make up the deficit in tax receipts, the
curiales were eventually destroyed. The end of the free farmer,
argued Westermann, also diminished intellectual vigor in the
agrarian population. He concluded that loss of economic
freedom, even more than loss of political freedom, undermined Graeco-Roman civilization. An economic interpretation
rooted in the capitalistic-liberal tradition of nineteenth-century

Europe, this explanation suffers from bias and from the application of nineteenth-century economic assumptions to the ancient world. It gives too exalted a role to the free farmer and
his influence on classical culture. Until the first century B.C.
the good fighters for the legions were mostly farmers, but long
before the first century, farmers had ceased to participate in
politics and had become quasi-professional warriors absent
for long periods from Italy and their farms. How can one prove
that they ever possessed intellectual vigor? The most one can
say is that in the earlier days of the republic they possessed
shrewdness and civic ardor. Westermann also fails to acknowledge that the large agrarian estates (*latifundia*) worked by
slaves were already in existence in the second century B.C., and
that this agrarian system continued into the late imperial
period when finally *coloni* were substituted for the depleted
slave labor. For almost five hundred years the republic and
empire had lived upon the *latifundia* worked by slaves or
dependent peasants. While there is no defense for this system of exploitation, there is also no justification to link it as
closely, as does Westermann, to the destruction of the ancient world. If its effects were as deleterious as he believed,
Rome could not have survived for five hundred years.

Inspired by Marxian economic thought, a number of economists and historians, among them K. Bücher (1847–1930),
Max Weber (1864–1920), and G. Salvioli (1857–1928), have
interpreted economic history as a succession of economies
progressively being replaced by those more highly developed. They felt the ancient world presented the example
of the most primitive economy, the house-economy, which
yielded in the Middle Ages to a higher economic level, the
city-economy, which in turn was superseded by the modern
state-economy, essentially capitalistic. Such an analysis is unfortunate because it forces economic development to fit
within a rigid pattern of Marxian dialectic. It also ignores
the facts. The economy of the ancient world was not simply
a house-economy but was in some cases a city-economy and
some forms of primitive capitalism were already practiced.
The medieval economy was not simply that of the city; it was
regional and international and moving toward that of a state-
economy. To apply economic labels to these periods of history
without serious analysis of the evidence and to insist upon a

line of continuous economic change from the primitive to the
more advanced, ending ultimately in a communistic economy,
is less than historical. Even more indefensible historically because it ignores the evidence and has the ring of a polemic is
Georges Sorel's (1847–1922) fervent attempt to explain the
sickness of the ancient world by means of Marxian ideology.
His vitriolic treatment of Christianity is ridiculous. By comparison, Gibbon's satirical and cynical attitude appears sympathetic!

Elaborating upon his theory that the ancient world had
a simple house-economy, Max Weber has emphasized that
it lived upon the labor of slaves and that when the slave
supply dried up, it died. He likened the supply of slave labor
to the supply of coal for an industrialized society where the
lack of coal would completely hobble the economy and lead
to that society's disintegration. That slavery was a prominent social and economic institution in the ancient world is
well known, but Weber has misunderstood its significance in
his desire to fit it into a model designed for explaining world
social and economic development. Before Rome emerged as a
great power, slavery provided much of the labor for the Mediterranean economy and remained prominent as a source of
labor into the second century A.D. when the depletion of
supply forced the substitution of free laborers, the *coloni*,
who eventually became economic dependents tied to the
land and placed in a hereditary caste, but never slaves. During part of the third, the fourth, and the fifth century,
therefore, the economy of the empire no longer rested upon
slave labor. Though it may be countered that the colonate and
caste system of Diocletian and Constantine were but forms
of forced labor hardly distinguishable from slavery, they were
only results of a long-standing economic malady.

Whether or not one agrees with Weber that a civilization
based upon slave labor cannot survive and must yield to one
supported by a more efficient, rational, and humane system
of labor and production, the thought arises that slave labor
may have so adversely influenced the classical world as to
doom its other considerable achievements. Believing this was
true, F. W. Walbank argued that slave labor prevented men
from seeing the benefits of technology (1953). With the whole
ancient economy geared to slave labor, there was no appli-

cation of theoretical mathematical and scientific knowledge to labor-saving machinery and power. Failure to develop industrial capacity in the West, an area always economically underdeveloped, forebode inevitable catastrophe. Lacking goods to exchange for eastern products, the West drained its liquid wealth and regressed. Distant trade diminished and the economy became regionalized, localized, and ultimately mostly self-sufficient and agrarian. Walbank affirms that classical civilization was condemned to failure because it compensated for "an absolutely low technique" with its "institution of slavery." [20] Tied to what he admits to be a deterministic argument is his further conclusion that this economic system perpetuated the bourgeoisie monopoly of power and that the bourgeoisie of the classical city-states never would have abdicated any of its power to the proletariat or to the slaves in an attempt to alleviate the blatant social, economic, and political injustices. Only the destruction of classical civilization could eradicate these evils in which lay the root of failure. What Walbank cannot answer is whether classical society was aware of the alternatives and, if so, whether it had the social and economic capacity to make the changes. This inability to face up to what was possible or whether what was possible would have had different historical effects is always a weakness of any explanation modeled upon the social and economic thought of Marx.

There are historians, like H. M. R. Leopold, who have contended that drastic state interference in and regulation of the economy only worsened the troubles of the empire (1918), but this observation rests mostly upon modern laissez-faire economic thought rather than ancient evidence. The rejoinder (1938) of F. Heichelheim that it was the duty of the state to intervene in the economy and that the policies of Diocletian and Constantine were efficacious seems to square better with the evidence. But Heichelheim must be reminded that this intervention only temporarily rescued the empire in the West, that state interference only postponed the collapse. The essential question is why such desperate measures were necessary.

One of the most convincing answers (1927) has been that of Ferdinand Lot. While attributing the end of the ancient world to a variety of complex causes, including psychological

20. Walbank, *Decline of Roman Empire,* p. 69.

alteration, he diagnoses much of the trouble as stemming from
a maladjusted economy. As he expressed it, "the Empire died
of an internal malady." The economy of the western part,
never well developed, remained essentially agrarian. Even in
Gaul, which did become well known for its brick and pottery
production, industrial enterprises were on a small scale. In
Rome, the largest city in the West, hardly any of the inhabitants engaged in productive enterprises such as industry or
trade. The aristocracy lived from the income of their estates.
What few aristocrats derived incomes from other sources engaged in activities like those of the *equites*, the middle class,
who were moneylenders or tax farmers. Essentially, the West
did not engage in trade or industry, living instead from the
land or from the profits of moneylending and tax collecting,
enterprises described by Lot as parasitical. The real centers of
industrial production and maritime commerce and the large
centers of population with economic and technological know-
how were in the East. For centuries the tribute and booty
exacted from the East, that is, its exploitation, brought tremendous, unearned wealth to the West which it lived upon
until eventually the unfavorable economic balance began to
have its effect. Unable to exploit the East indefinitely, especially
after it had been incorporated and organized into provinces, the
West began to deplete its wealth. To pay for products fabri-
cated in the East and to pay those from the East who traded
in and transported them, the West had to use the money origi-
nally extorted from the East. What it could sell in exchange
did not begin to pay for the eastern purchases and there developed a severe imbalance of trade that ultimately drained
the West of its wealth. As a result, the East, with its more
highly developed economy, survived the political and military
troubles of the fourth and fifth centuries while the West sank
deeper into an agrarian economy that resulted in political collapse, the disappearance of technical and artistic skills, and
the decay of learning. A shrewd analysis of the economic
shortcomings of the empire in the West, Lot's theory has been
strengthened by other scholars. The Byzantinist Norman H.
Baynes (1877–1961) has argued that the economy of the East
enabled the eastern empire to support the organs of government and to maintain the military forces necessary to defend

the frontiers against the Germans, Persians, and Arabs, while "it was the pitiful poverty of Western Rome which crippled her in her effort to maintain that civil and military system which was the presupposition for the continued life of the ancient civilisation." [21] Marc Bloch (1886–1944) in a study of the numismatic evidence has concluded that there was a virtual hemorrhage of gold from West to East resulting in the deep economic troubles of the West.

A fascinating social-economic interpretation of the imperial malady has been elucidated by Michael Rostovtzeff (1870–1952) in his masterly *Social and Economic History of the Roman Empire.* He regarded the towns (*municipia*) as the means by which Rome unified Italy and by which she Romanized the vast conquered territory around the Mediterranean. Essentially the health of the empire depended upon its towns. Because the towns drew their wealth from the countryside, this meant, according to Rostovtzeff, the exploitation of the peasantry by the bourgeoisie of the towns, resulting in tension between them. During the long *Pax Romana* the bourgeoisie became so unaccustomed to and unfitted for military service that in the crises of the third century the Roman armies were largely recruited from the rude and vigorous peasantry. At this point the peasantry in the army made common cause with that still on the land and waged a war of extermination against the hated bourgeoisie. The extermination of those who for centuries had governed, who were educated and cultured, and who had a monopoly of talent and experience brought an end to classical civilization. This analysis led Rostovtzeff to conclude that "violent attempts at levelling have never helped to uplift the masses. They have destroyed the upper classes, and resulted in accelerating the process of barbarization. But the ultimate problem remains like a ghost, ever present and unlaid: Is it possible to extend a higher civilization to the lower classes without debasing its standard and diluting its quality to the vanishing point? Is not every civilization bound to decay as soon as it begins to penetrate the masses?" [22]

21. Baynes, "The Decline of the Roman Power in Western Europe. Some Modern Explanations," *Journal of Roman Studies,* XXXIII (1943), 35.

22. Rostovtzeff, *The Social and Economic History of the Roman Empire,* p. 487.

Such questions pose tantalizing problems because they strike at the roots of fundamental issues that puzzle man. In linking the health of the Roman Empire to its *municipia,* Rostovtzeff was right. They were, in truth, a microcosm of the empire and its pulse. When they became sick, the whole body took on the sickness and died. But did these *municipia* die from the illness diagnosed by Rostovtzeff? His proposition that a civilization rests upon educated, cultured, and talented people with experience is sound, but how does a civilization assure itself an adequate supply of such people? If a privileged class becomes too exclusive is it not in danger of withering from lack of talent as well as of causing bitterness and class hatred? Does the extension of privilege and culture downward necessarily mean the dilution of excellence and achievement? Although such questions are still debated, the experience of modern society indicates that a culture does not decay when privilege and education are open to all. But was the ancient world ready for all men to share in its culture? Perhaps not. Even Christianity, despite its humanitarian doctrines, did not alter class distinction or eliminate privilege; instead it supported class and hierarchical authority and became the bedrock of the medieval belief in the divinely ordered three estates. Whatever one's reactions to these sensitive questions, he must realize that Rostovtzeff, the Russian bourgeois intellectual from St. Petersburg, was completely unsympathetic to the Russian Revolution of 1917 and the subsequent Bolshevik regime. Emigrating to the United States where he obtained an academic post, he pondered the events in Russia and clearly applied what he had experienced and observed to solving the decline of the ancient world. His magisterial history therefore sadly lacks objectivity and most of the evidence simply does not substantiate his thesis. There is no proof, for example, that the peasant in the army joined forces with the peasant of the countryside in a war of extermination of the urban bourgeoisie. This is what occurred in Russia! Criticizing Rostovtzeff, Baynes has concluded: "I have consulted every reference to the authorities cited by Professor Rostovtzeff and in my judgment none of them supports his reading of the facts." [23]

23. Baynes, *Journal of Roman Studies,* XXXIII, 34.

HISTORICAL CONTINGENCY

While most scholars have thought it possible to pin-
point some cause or group of causes for the decline of the
ancient world, a minority have despaired of locating any one
cause or of being able to construct a general theory. Typical of
this minority is J. B. Bury (1861–1927) who dismisses the
German invasions, decline of population, the disintegrating
influence of Christianity, and other explanations and declares
that the success of the barbarians in occupying the West can
be accounted for only by knowledge of actual events. He is
convinced that "the gradual collapse of the Roman power in
this section of the Empire was the consequence of *a series of
contingent events.* No general causes can be assigned that
made it inevitable." [24] Among the contingencies Bury finds
responsible for Rome's loss of her provinces in the fifth century
were the irruption of the Huns into Europe, the defeat and
death at Adrianople in 378 of the emperor Valens at the hands
of the Visigoths, the inopportune death of Valens's successor,
the subsequent rule of a feebleminded boy, and the policies
of Stilicho that led to civil war. Bury may be right in saying
that too little importance has been accorded actual events
surrounding the end of the empire in the West, but why should
a few military reverses, a number of unfortunate deaths, some
ill-starred political decisions, and the brief rule of an incompetent youth be enough to kill off an empire? Had it not
already been in serious trouble, these events might not have
occurred, or if they had, would certainly not have had the
consequences ascribed to them by Bury. To exclude luck in
history as explaining certain events or developments would be
foolish, but luck as a prime force of historical causation serves
the modern historian no better than did *fortuna* the Roman
historian Tacitus. Basically in accord with Bury, R. M. Haywood, poking fun at scholars for attempting to date the fall of
Rome, has concluded (1958) that it was due to no one cause
and that it is useless to draw any lessons for the modern world.

If an attempt were made to place the above interpretations, theories, and explanations in chronological perspective,
most would be found to have appeared between 1890 and

24. Bury, *History of the Later Roman Empire, 395–565,* I, 309.

1930. Interesting also is that at least ninety percent came from the pens of classical historians. Few medievalists, it seems, asked why the ancient world ended when it ended, or when the Middle Ages began. Most, content to leave the debate to the classical historians and to accept their conclusions, regarded the fourth or fifth century as the proper starting point of the Middle Ages and invariably addressed themselves first to the invasions of the Germans (*Völkerwanderung*) and to the barbarous customs and institutions of these strangers to Graeco-Roman culture. Except for refinement of explanations and a more sophisticated study of the sources, Gibbon's interpretation was little modified. If he could have sat again in the Roman Forum in the 1920's and studied the revisions to his work, he would have been agreeably surprised. There was application of modern social and economic history, a more sympathetic and objective attitude toward Christianity, and a greater appreciation of artistic developments, but little else that was revised or added. He would have found that the social and economic explanations supported his conclusions that the empire in the West ended in the fourth century and, while he might have been unhappy with modern scholarly appreciation of Christianity, he would soon have realized that it did not change his interpretation. Having accused the Christian faith of incubating a psychology of docility, retreat, contemplation, theological discord, and supreme devotion to a spiritual ruler, he would learn that modern scholarship also believed Christianity to have been responsible for a collective attitude different from that of Graeco-Roman civilization; a psychology that created a new morality, a new individualism, a new concept of man's relation to the universe, a new explanation of man's existence and his fate after death, and a new attitude toward the nature and proper objective of learning; all of which mental, emotional, and spiritual transformations revolutionized western history during the fourth and fifth centuries and ushered in the Middle Ages and a new western civilization. Departing from the Roman Forum this time, Gibbon could justifiably congratulate himself for writing a book that had withstood the test of time, even as his acute mind set him to pondering why historians had been so content with his interpretation, why they had been so little inclined to doubt or challenge it.

3. Pirenne to the Present

Such was the state of historiography on this problem in the 1920's. As yet no historian, classical or medieval, had challenged the humanist-enlightenment-Gibbonesque explanation or doubted that the ancient world ended in the fourth or fifth century. Even historians like the distinguished French medievalist Fustel de Coulanges (1830–1889), the leader of the Romanist school of historiography, were only concerned with proving that some of the institutions of the ancient world survived beyond the fifth century. Fustel established that Roman institutions influenced the development of early medieval institutions in France, Alfons Dopsch (1868–1953) supported this view, but with exaggerated conclusions; and other historians, such as Christopher Dawson, began to emphasize the medieval debt to classical culture via the Christian church which served as the bridge between the ancient world and the Middle Ages (1932). These were, however, but slight beginnings of a revisionist movement that failed to shake confidence in Gibbon's monument. Not until after World War I was this scholarly consensus disturbed by a new interpretation, questioning most of what historians had accepted as faith since the Renaissance. The challenge came not from a classical historian but from a Belgian medievalist, Henri Pirenne (1862–1935), who advanced a theory on the end of the ancient world and the beginning of the Middle Ages that upset traditional belief and provided the conceptual framework for all subsequent discussion of the problem.

PIRENNE'S THESIS

Before World War I there is little evidence that Henri Pirenne had especially concerned himself with the problem of when the Middle Ages began, although he was vitally interested in the early Middle Ages. He had studied first at the University of Liège with the eminent medievalist Godefroid Kurth, an authority on Merovingian France and early medieval culture and Christianity, and later in Paris and in Germany with other specialists in early medieval history. He was thoroughly informed of the Germanist-Romanist debates over early medieval institutions. In his research on seignorialism he often agreed with the conclusions of Fustel de Coulanges, whose lectures at the Sorbonne he had regularly attended. From his increased interest in the origin and significance of the medieval town, he gradually mastered early medieval social, economic, and institutional history. In the 1890's he wrote classic articles in *La Revue Historique* criticizing the theories propounded on town origins and advancing his celebrated mercantilist-settlement theory. He attacked those historians who derived the medieval town from Roman origins, who believed that Roman *civitates* and legionary camps survived throughout the early Middle Ages and provided the basis for the renewed urban life of western Europe in the late tenth and eleventh centuries. He dealt even more severely with Germanist historians who derived the town from what he considered to be mythical early German agrarian communities of free peasants. Convinced that towns decayed along with the disintegration of the Roman Empire in the West and that true urban life did not reappear until there was economic revival, he regarded the medieval town as a new social and economic phenomenon created by the economic revival of western Europe during the late tenth and eleventh centuries and therefore disavowed Romanist and Germanist explanations. At this stage of his research he was concerned with the end of the empire in the West only as it spelled the disappearance of towns and did not probe deeper into when and why the ancient world died. His lectures delivered during this time at the University of Ghent occasionally hinted at his dissatisfaction with the answers to these questions but generally embodied no serious questioning of the traditional interpretations. He obviously rejected Gibbon's biased charges against early Christianity and was perfectly aware that the Germans did not abruptly and brutally destroy the western empire in the fourth and fifth centuries because he emphasized that the empire had serious problems prior to the fourth century, that its culture and institutions were deteriorating, and that this decline extended over a long period of time; but his views stopped here until 1914.

The outbreak of World War I and the occupation of Belgium by German troops was a dramatic watershed in Pirenne's life that brought personal loss and sorrow to his family, disrupted his academic routine, closed the University of Ghent, and eventually made him a prisoner deep in Germany. As a leader of the faculty opposing the policies of the occupation authorities to Germanize the curriculum of the University of Ghent, Pirenne together with another colleague was arrested without warning on 18 March 1916 and deported to Germany where he remained until the end of war in November 1918. When, during his stay of four months at the prison camp of Holzminden, he was asked by numerous prisoners to give a series of lectures in history, he responded by lecturing on Belgian history for his fellow Belgians and on the social and economic history of medieval Europe for a large group of Russians and others. For the first time he began to think specifically about the end of the ancient world and to experiment with various of his ideas. It is also apparent that his contact with the Russians and his acquisition of a reading knowledge of the Russian language broadened his perspective of European history and gave him new insights into Byzantine and middle eastern history. After internment at two prison camps and residence for a short period in the university town of Jena, he was sent to Creuzburg-an-der-Werra, a small Thuringian town with a population of approximately two thousand, where, terribly alone and the sole alien, he remained until the war ended. Although he continued his study of Russian, read extensively, and followed a routine that included long daily walks, he soon realized that he needed more to sustain him. As he wrote in his diary, "I decided immediately that I could never hold out against the monotony of my detention unless

I forced myself to undertake some definite occupation. . . .
In short, I understood, or at least I think I did understand,
the voluntary seclusion of Descartes in 'his room with a Dutch
stove.' " [25] It was then that Pirenne decided to expand the
lectures given at Holzminden, then that he embarked upon a
history of Europe. With comparatively few books at his disposal he began, writing two pages each day, and had taken
his account to 1550 when the war ended and he was free to
return to Belgium.

Immersed once more in his teaching and other writing,
Pirenne never again worked on this manuscript, but it was
published posthumously in 1936 under the title *Histoire de
l'Europe des invasions au XVIᵉ siècle*. What definitely
emerges from this work is that Pirenne began to revise his
conceptions of the early Middle Ages in 1917 and 1918. What
essentially took shape in his mind was an ancient world that
was for some centuries in decline but that was not destroyed
by the Germans except for the end of the political existence
of the empire in the West. He perceived that the Germans
did not arrive in the empire as enemies but as men who
wished to enjoy and partake of its superior culture and to preserve all that they could. Though incapable of preserving
much, they did, within their limitations, adopt and continue
Roman culture and institutions, thereby prolonging for some
time the essential ingredients of ancient civilization. Pirenne
concluded that the Germans "had no hatred of Rome and
. . . did not maltreat the population," that their "kingdoms
were Roman not merely because the Roman civilization had
furnished them with the framework within which, and thanks
to which, they had succeeded in organizing themselves, but
also because they *wished* to be Roman." [26] Pirenne was, however, under no illusion that the ancient world was not in
decline. He was aware that western Europe presented a spec-
tacle not of youth but of "the decadence of Imperial civilization," that the sixth-century bishop Gregory of Tours perfectly
summed it up with the discouraged words *"mundus senescit*
(the world grows old)." [27]

25. Pirenne, *A History of Europe*, I, xxviii–xxix. For an excellent
account of Pirenne's captivity, see his *Souvenirs de captivité en Allemagne*
(Brussels, 1921).
26. *Ibid.*, p. 16.
27. *Ibid.*, p. 17.

So intrigued had Pirenne become with this problem that shortly after the war in 1922 and 1923 he further articulated his ideas on it in two articles bearing the suggestive titles "Mahomet et Charlemagne" and "Un contraste économique: Mérovingiens et Carolingiens" which led him to investigate the decline of the ancient world in all its aspects and to publish the results in a series of articles. In 1928 at the International Congress of Historical Sciences at Oslo he presented his ideas in a well-formulated thesis before the assembled historians. When he died in 1935, on his desk was the first draft of a manuscript entitled *Mahomet et Charlemagne* that was prepared for publication in 1937 by his son Jacques, also a historian, and a former student, Fernand Vercauteren. Here Pirenne elucidated his celebrated theory on the end of the ancient world and the beginning of the Middle Ages.

Dramatically breaking with Gibbon's interpretation, Pirenne sparked the first scholarly reexamination of the problem since the Enlightenment by asserting that the ancient world did not end until the Arab conquests of the seventh and eighth centuries had swept around three sides of the Mediterranean, converting it into a Moslem lake on which, as one later Arab historian graphically wrote, the Christians could no longer "float a plank." Achieved, according to Pirenne, by the last quarter of the eighth century, this Arab dominance of the Mediterranean had destroyed the essential nature or quality of the ancient classical world embodied in its unity and coherence, resting upon control of the Mediterranean from the Bosphorus to the Strait of Gibraltar. For centuries the *Mare Nostrum* of the Romans, over whose waters had passed the essential trade and the Roman military and naval might, had been the cement that had held together the huge imperial structure. As a boulevard for the vital exchange of ideas, it bound together Graeco-Roman civilization. This strategic Mediterranean component of the Roman Empire had not, argued Pirenne, been destroyed by the German tribes that occupied the provinces of the western empire. Instead, they admired and worked to sustain the Mediterranean civilization to which they had been introduced. Some of the German chiefs mimicked the Roman emperors in dress and ceremony, appropriated titles for themselves and their officials, and utilized the institutions of Roman government like the *civitas,* which continued as a center of administration. The gold shilling of Diocletian and Constantine (*solidus*) remained in use and was, in fact, a symbol of the economic continuity between the Romans and the Germans. They were less successful in preserving classical culture, but some of the German kings, most notably those of the Ostrogoths and the Visigoths, showed an appreciation of Latin letters and thought, of art and architecture. They also patronized intellectuals and artists, even using some of them as officials. Moreover, the Germans were converted to Christianity which facilitated their Romanization. Though the new German kingdoms had tenuous ties with the eastern empire, some of their kings continued to act as though in some sense they were viceroys of the emperors in Constantinople. But most striking of all is that the Germans were drawn to the Mediterranean physically and psychologically, they partook eagerly of the Mediterranean unity, and they enjoyed unbroken economic relations with the East.

With the Arab conquests, all this ended; political, economic, and cultural relations ceased. Except for precarious relations between Constantinople and a few Italian ports such as Venice, Amalfi, and Bari, the Arabs rolled down a curtain between East and West that remained down until the eleventh century. Thereafter, it was the Crescent versus the Cross. The West, formerly parasitical, living upon the superior economic resources of the East, now swiftly reverted to an agrarian economy or, as Pirenne expressed it, to "an economy of no outlets." Monopolizing the Mediterranean, the Arabs pushed western Europe away from its shores so that the Carolingian state of the eighth and ninth centuries became landlocked. Political organization meanwhile became primitive, true urban life disappeared as trade withered, and culture receded and became stagnant. Men subsisted from the land by a system of economic exploitation known as seignorialism and provided for the fundamental military and political needs of their primitive society by developing the feudal system. From necessity, political and military power gravitated northward above the Alps where it was to remain for centuries, and where were to center the principal developments of medieval civilization and of that culture and those institutions peculiarly western. As Pirenne wrote in a memorable passage: "It is therefore strictly correct to say that without Mohammed Charlemagne would have been inconceivable. In the 7th century the ancient Roman Empire had actually become an Empire of the East; the Empire of Charles was an Empire of the West. . . . The Carolingian Empire, or rather, the Empire of Charlemagne, was the scaffolding of the Middle Ages." [28] The coronation of Charlemagne as emperor by Pope Leo III on Christmas Day 800 in the basilica of St. Peter in Rome symbolized for Pirenne the end of the ancient world and the beginning of the medieval.

Pirenne's theory is provocative. It postpones the end of the ancient world in the West until the eighth century and hinges imperial survival and, with it, Graeco-Roman civilization upon control of the Mediterranean. If valid, it nullifies most previous explanations or debilitates their strongest arguments. Controversial and dramatic, it stunned, infuriated, or excited historians and refocussed the attention of numerous medievalists on this important period of transition. In describing the buzz of historians in the rooms and corridors after listening to Pirenne's dramatic paper in Oslo, Lucien Febvre caught the spirit of excitement that was engendered. Pirenne forced historians to reexamine the whole problem and to question the conceptual framework that had dominated historical thinking since the Renaissance. Spurred to research and writing by this unorthodox theory, historians ever since have been busily appraising it; few historical theories of the nineteenth and twentieth centuries have aroused more interest or caused more debate. Our task now is to see how Pirenne's ideas have stood the criticism of the past thirty-five years.

GERMAN INVASIONS AND RELATED PROBLEMS

Such scholars as Fustel de Coulanges, Alfons Dopsch, Ferdinand Lot, and Pirenne have convinced most historians that the German conquests were not a sudden catastrophe for western Europe, abruptly ending classical civilization, and introducing centuries of "Gothic barbarism." But some historians have refused to change their chronology,

28. Pirenne, *Mohammed and Charlemagne*, pp. 234–235.

holding firmly to the fourth and fifth centuries as the beginning of the Middle Ages, even though conceding that frag-
ments of classical civilization survived the Germans' entry into
the empire. Labelling these centuries a sort of *Uebergangs-
zone* (transitional period), Hermann Aubin insists that the
Germans brought with them new conceptions that trans-
formed political institutions, the law, classical thought, and
the church, all of which wrought fundamental cultural and
psychological changes. According to Emilienne Demougeot,
the German invasions had so disrupted Roman unity by 410
that thereafter one must speak of the *pars Orientis* and the
pars Occidentis, with the latter ceasing rapidly to be Roman
as the German kingdoms established themselves. Others, including Lot and the majority of English scholars, agree with
Louis Halphen that the invasions completely upset the world,
that it was no longer ancient, but medieval. H. St. L. B. Moss
marks the end of the ancient world with the death of the
emperor Theodosius in 395 because he was the last emperor
to rule over East and West. J. M. Wallace-Hadrill is convinced
that Odoacer's deposition of Romulus Augustulus in 476 is the
key event because "the chroniclers of the time show an aware-
ness that something bigger had happened." [29] Pirenne would
not wholly disagree with these appraisals of events in the
fourth and fifth centuries; as suggested earlier, he never held
that the Roman Empire was in good shape after the third
century. His view was that although *Romania* had suffered in
the northern provinces, it "still survived as a whole. It had, of
course, altered greatly for the worse. In every domain of life,
in the arts, literature and science, the regression is mani-
fest." [30] Well aware of the repercussions of the Germans,
Pirenne was not convinced that they were catastrophic
enough to destroy completely the ancient world. Most medievalists would agree. To ascertain the opinion of classical historians, however, is more difficult because so few seemed to
realize that Pirenne's theory places in question so many of
their traditional interpretations of late imperial history. Perhaps typical is A. H. M. Jones who regards as causes of imperial collapse in the West the barbarian attacks, loss of public

29. Wallace-Hadrill, *The Barbarian West, 400–1000,* p. 32.
30. Pirenne, *Mohammed and Charlemagne,* p. 45.

spirit, and a corrupt bureaucracy. His concept of decline emerges from his comment upon the sack of Rome in 410 by Alaric: "The fall of Rome spelt the fall of the Empire; it even meant the end of the world." [31] Is this not essentially what Gibbon argued?

Some historians have been even less prone than Pirenne to ascribe major significance to the German movement into the West. They have argued that by the end of the second century the empire began to weaken and that by the fourth century its social, economic, and political institutions were so debilitated as to invite the Germans to move into the provinces and settle there. These historians, with a stance resembling that of Rostovtzeff, would place the end of the ancient world after the reign of Constantine (306–337). Some medievalists, on the other hand, have regarded the Germans simply as catalysts who so seriously disrupted the economy in the West during the fourth and fifth centuries that what was left of classical culture quickly vanished. They would therefore place the end of the ancient world considerably later than Constantine. Representative of these historians, G. I. Bratianu sees the German invasions as furnishing fuel to an economic decline long in progress, and he believes that the Arab conquests only served to place the finishing touches to this economic decline so obvious since Diocletian. He cites Roman evidence to the effect that "the rural bases of the western economy were the product of a very ancient history." [32] P. C. Roberts has also attributed economic consequences to the Germans. Addressing himself particularly to Gaul, he finds that the invasions affected the volume of trade there, that they hastened "the process of passage from the uniform imperial economic organization to an economy of local production and barter." He contends that the economy of Gaul was almost exclusively that of provisioner of Rome, and that when the Germans disrupted this economic relation the West was in serious trouble because "all economic trade was purposely oriented by Rome towards Rome. Thus, Rome was the con-

31. Jones, *The Later Roman Empire 284–602. A Social, Economic and Administrative Survey,* II, 1025.
32. Bratianu, *Etudes byzantines d'histoire économique et sociale,* p. 86.

centration into a few square miles of the resources of a whole empire." [33] Pirenne would mostly agree with this school of thought, but instead of considering the economic crisis to be as critical in the fourth and fifth centuries as did Bratianu, he envisions a more gentle and gradual economic decline climaxed by the Arabs in the seventh and eighth centuries. Contemplating the period from Diocletian to the Merovingian king Dagobert (639), Pirenne wrote that "the constitution of society was predominantly agrarian" but insisted that "it was not exclusively so. Commerce and towns still played a considerable part in the general economic, social and intellectual life of the age." [34]

CULTURE, RELIGION, AND INSTITUTIONS

Because Pirenne rested his theory upon the unity of the Mediterranean, a unity that sustained the economy of the ancient world, he was less concerned with cultural and religious history, thereby becoming vulnerable to the charge of neglecting vital cultural and spiritual change. Those critical of Pirenne on this score paint a decline of classical literature and art, an abandonment of pagan gods and philosophy, and an aridity of creative endeavor that combined to make the fourth and fifth centuries a watershed and produced a new mentality and spiritual outlook which nurtured those qualities associated with the medieval mind. This position has been eloquently stated by Christopher Dawson, with support from others such as C. Delisle Burns. What is striking, however, is that Dawson, although concentrating upon thought and letters, should emerge with conclusions similar to those of Pirenne. He attaches great significance to the Arab conquests of the seventh century, asserting that "it is in the seventh century, and not in the fifth, that we must place the end of the last phase of ancient Mediterranean civilization—the age of the Christian empire—and the beginnings of the Middle

---

33. Roberts, "The Pirenne Thesis, Economies or Civilizations, Towards Reformulation," *Classica et Mediaevalia*, XXV (1964), 306, 311.
34. Pirenne, *Mohammed and Charlemagne*, p. 79.

Ages." [35] Like Pirenne, Dawson interprets the coronation of Charlemagne as emperor in 800 as inaugurating a new age because it brought final fusion of the classical, the Christian, and the Germanic elements upon which medieval western civilization was to develop. Henceforth, Dawson contends, culture regarded as typically western and European was to arise in the north between the Loire and Rhine rivers.

Although emphasizing different causes and forces responsible for the inauguration of the Middle Ages, Pirenne and Dawson surprisingly agree on fundamental issues. But there is sharp disagreement between Pirenne and recent disciples of Dawson who enthusiastically attribute a dynamic character to the period between the fifth and ninth centuries, a period Pirenne considered progressively decadent and inactive. Granted that there is much to be done in the cultural and religious history of this remote and difficult period and that Pirenne was not enough attentive to such history and did not have sufficient sympathy or understanding for it, we can rightfully ask for more evidence from those like W. C. Bark who believe that this period witnessed the release of dynamic new forces, that it was "the seedbed" of our "legacy of freedom and dignity," of the equality of women, and of the rights of labor. The evidence presented so far does not justify such a picture of these centuries.

For the period prior to the seventh century Pirenne's theory is not in conflict with the theory of continuity supported by members of the Romanist school such as Dopsch and Robert Latouche, but after the seventh century there is an intellectual no-man's-land. Dopsch and his comrades, despite acknowledgement of a temporary and serious slump in the economy caused by the Arab sweep and later, during the ninth century, by the Vikings, still insist upon an institutional continuity dating back to the Roman Empire. They are convinced that Roman institutions, especially urban and agrarian, weakened but somehow clung on until the eleventh century when conditions improved and became the foundation and stimulation for the famous political, economic, social, and cultural rebirth that swept over western Europe. Dopsch

35. Dawson, *The Making of Europe. An Introduction to the History of European Unity*, p. 136.

thought he had proved that "this period of the fifth and sixth centuries is seen to be the organic and vital connecting link between late Roman and Carolingian times."[36] Subsequently, in a study of the economic history of the Low Countries, Renée Doehaerd drew a picture of economic expansion as a continuous phenomenon from the late Roman period to the end of the tenth century.

In general accord on social and economic conditions in the Merovingian period, Dopsch broke with Pirenne on the Carolingian period. Where Pirenne considered it the lowest point of the western economy prior to the revival in the eleventh century, Dopsch saw in it signs of economic improvement, especially during the reign of Charlemagne. He saw an increase in local and regional markets; the rise of trade along such waterways as the Rhine, Meuse, and Scheldt; the clearing of land for additional cultivation; and a growth in agrarian productivity. He concluded from study of the Carolingian capitularies, particularly that of the *Capitulare de villis,* that Charlemagne was vitally concerned with economic conditions and adopted policies designed to encourage greater agrarian productivity and efficiency; that the collective thrust of Charlemagne's efforts was toward achieving order, justice, and security in his realm for all subjects—conditions upon which economic progress rests. The recent study of F. L. Ganshof on Frankish institutions under Charlemagne, though not concerned with Carolingian social and economic history, indirectly supports the thesis of Dopsch by suggesting that Charlemagne in his so-called Programmatic Capitulary of 802 hoped to promote in his realm those conditions which underlie social and economic progress—peace, concord, efficient institutions, good justice, and trust in the ruler and his officials.

Latouche, a disciple of the Dopsch position, interprets continuity differently. Contrary to Dopsch and Pirenne, he sees the Merovingian period as that in which continuity came closest to being snapped. Referring to "the muddled, spineless Merovingian world of the sixth century," he argues that it affords the best evidence of the serious consequences of the German invasions of the fourth and fifth centuries and "of the inertia of the western peoples and of the stagnation of their

36. Dopsch, *The Economic and Social Foundations of European Civilization,* p. 390.

economic life." [37] Skeptical of Pirenne's picture of Merovingian economic activity and its role in the economic unity of
the Mediterranean, he interprets the Carolingian period as a
temporary restoration of the western economy. The Carolingian efforts at revival, described as a controlled economy and
reform of the coinage, were dashed by the Viking raids and
invasions of the ninth century, but fortunately this disruption
was only temporary. By the tenth century the Vikings had
ceased their raids and piracy and had channeled their magnificent seafaring talents into trading. Dominating the northern
seas, they stimulated the economy of those lands bordering the
Atlantic, Baltic, and North Sea and linked the West to the
East by way of the route going east to Novgorod and then
south to Kiev and along the Dnieper River down to Constantinople. Although differing with Pirenne on the Carolingian
economy, Latouche is in closer rapport in his evaluation of
events in the late ninth and early tenth centuries. Both appre-
ciated the role of the Vikings as stimulators of the western
economy, following the cessation of their activity as pirates
and raiders, and Pirenne compared their role in the north to
that of Venice in the south. Latouche believes Pirenne was
justified in assigning the Arabs a major part in the emergence
of western Christendom, but not in portraying the ancient
world as continuing until the Arabs swept into the Mediterranean. He believes that a break almost came in the Merovingian period. Perceiving signs of promise in the Carolingian
economy, he is also convinced that Pirenne's dark portrait too
much resembles Gibbon's sardonic description of Charlemagne as preoccupied with "the care of his poultry and even
with the sale of his eggs." [38]

While an antidote to the Germanist position that the Middle Ages began with the Germans and were founded upon
German institutions, the extreme Romanist position has been
so discredited as to preclude further discussion. Let us ask,
instead, why the interpretations of Pirenne, Dopsch, and Latouche so sharply diverge. Why should Pirenne, a moderate
Romanist, disagree in many respects with the more committed
Romanists Dopsch and Latouche when all three studied the

37. Latouche, *The Birth of Western Economy*, pp. 120, 123.
38. Gibbon, *Decline and Fall of the Roman Empire* (ed. J. B. Bury),
V, 285.

same evidence? According to some scholars this question cannot be answered without intensive, almost minute study of the economic evidence of the Merovingian and Carolingian periods to see how much trade there actually was in the two periods. Those historians loath to prolong the ancient world beyond the fifth century find the debate for Merovingian and Carolingian trade irrelevant. They feel that if economic conditions caused the end of the ancient world, then examine those conditions in the third, fourth, and fifth centuries! Norman H. Baynes, for instance, would support Rostovtzeff's position that trade throughout the Mediterranean declined in the late imperial period but that the crucial point came with the Germans, especially the Vandals, who, from their strategic position in northern Africa across from Sicily, blocked trade between East and West, thus destroying the economic unity of the Mediterranean. To "state that for the Franks of the sixth century the Mediterranean still remained '*mare nostrum*'" is therefore inaccurate; the Vandals had "marooned" the Merovingians from the eastern empire.[39] Thereafter when the Merovingians obtained eastern goods, it was by way of imperial territory in Spain or Africa—after their reconquest by the eastern emperor Justinian—but never by direct exchange. In pointing to the Vandals as a cause for a break in normal East-West trade relations, Baynes is correct; but it was not a long and permanent break. Little different from the Franks, Ostrogoths, and Visigoths, the Vandals had no reason for living permanently upon piracy and soon cast their lot with the Mediterranean. Also, because their kingdom was so ephemeral and incorporated so soon into Justinian's renewed empire, their influence on Mediterranean trade could not have been decisive. The Vandals were but a brief inconvenience.

MEROVINGIAN AND CAROLINGIAN TRADE

How valid, nevertheless, is Pirenne's thesis that East-West trade relations continued in the Merovingian pe-

39. Baynes, "M. Pirenne and the Unity of the Mediterranean World," in *Byzantine Studies and Other Studies* (London, 1955), pp. 310–316. See also *Journal of Roman Studies*, XVIII (1929), 232.

riod? Some historians, among them Gunnar Mickwitz, Henri Laurent, Pierre Lambrechts, André Dupont, and Solomon Katz, disagree with Pirenne's evaluation of Jewish and Syrian merchants in the trade of the western Mediterranean. Although in accord with him that such merchants dominated international trade, they contend that their presence in the West is no guarantee that Mediterranean commerce continued much as it had prior to the arrival of the Germans. Some think that if only Jews and Syrians participated in trade, it indicates that most merchants had disappeared in the West. Others point out that Jews and Syrians had lived in Provence and Spain before the arrival of the Germans and that their presence does not necessarily argue for their role as intermediaries in international commerce. Concluding that the economy of western Europe in the Merovingian period was dormant and remained so until the revival in the eleventh century, these historians have ignored the Carolingian period. On the contrary, Dopsch and his enthusiastic student Erna Patzelt see economic improvement in the Merovingian period over the late imperial with a monetary economy based upon international trade. This optimistic view of continuity, although buttressing his position, was never shared by Pirenne. Never did he argue that economic conditions improved under the Merovingians, but only that the unity of the Mediterranean continued.

A large group of historians, apparently convinced there was some kind of continuity in the Merovingian period, has tried to determine whether the Arab invasions truly ended Mediterranean unity and resulted in a landlocked Carolingian state. Some who have limited their investigations to northern Europe, most notably A. R. Lewis, R. S. Lopez, D. Jellema, and J. Brutzkus, have even concluded that while trade underwent crises during the Viking period of piracy and invasion and during the anarchy that wrecked the Carolingian Empire after Charlemagne, long-distance trade never disappeared but was even rejuvenated by the Vikings and Frisians, that professional merchants maintained commercial contacts not only along the inland waterways of the Carolingian state but between England and the Continent, in the Baltic and North seas, and eastward to Russia where routes led to Byzantium and the Arab caliphate. This is certainly not a picture of a landlocked western Europe shut off from the East or dormant in its own regional trade.

Because Pirenne's argument rests primarily upon the effect of the Arabs on the Mediterranean economy, historians have reexamined the evidence used by him as well as evidence unknown to him or not then available. References in the Merovingian texts to spices, oil, silks, incense, jewelry, papyrus, and other eastern products indicated to Pirenne continuation of international trade, just as lack of such references in the Carolingian texts led him to conclude that the Arabs had cut off trade with the East. Some historians have, however, shown the existence of such goods in western Europe in the period between 700 and 1100. Typical of these historians are R. S. Lopez and Etienne Sabbe. The latter, a student of Pirenne, concluded that in the Carolingian and post-Carolingian periods a well-organized trade provided western Europe not only with silk but with a variety of *objets d'art*. He noted that trade routes crisscrossed the lands of western Europe and that there were maritime connections between the West and the East. He believed, moreover, that he encountered professional merchants in western Europe who were neither Jews nor Syrians. Lopez, not finding as much evidence for silks, incense, and spices as did Sabbe, ingeniously explained this lack as resulting from more frugal and simple tastes fostered by the primitive agrarian economy of the Carolingian period. Because only the church and a few aristocrats had the need or taste for luxury goods, the importation of such products decreased. Lopez also showed that papyrus from Egypt was used in the West long after Pirenne declared it to have been replaced by parchment. He found papyrus in use by the papacy until the middle of the eleventh century and in use for private documents to the end of the tenth century. It would seem, therefore, that the Arabs did not prevent the sale of papyrus and that it ceased to be used only when paper replaced it throughout the Arab world during the tenth century.

Lopez has, in addition, questioned Pirenne's analysis of coinage reform under Charlemagne. Noting that instead of striking the gold shilling, which had been the standard coin of exchange since Diocletian, Charlemagne struck only the silver *denarius* (penny) at the ratio of 240 to a pound, Pirenne concluded that trade between East and West had halted and that Charlemagne had substituted the penny to handle the minimal trade requirements of the agrarian West. As he so aptly expressed it, "The monetary system of Charles constituted a complete break with the Mediterranean economy which had continued until the invasion of Islam. . . . The new system of silver monometallism corresponded with the state of economic regression." [40] He suggested that the gold coins found after the reform of Charlemagne were stray ones that had filtered in from Byzantine and Arab lands by way of raids and piracy. Lopez challenges this explanation. He contends that Charlemagne changed over to a silver coinage with a more modest inscription merely to conciliate the Byzantine rulers who believed that only they had the legal right to mint gold coins with the inscription *Romanorum imperator*. In Italy, where the level of economic activity did not justify the abandonment of gold, Arabic and Byzantine gold coins continued in use. Lopez concluded, therefore, that "Charlemagne's monetary reforms were not prompted by the progress of Arab invasions, but, primarily, by considerations of good-neighbor policy towards the Byzantine Empire." [41]

Pirenne has also come under attack on other fronts. Charles Verlinden, another of his students and an authority on medieval slavery, has shown that Verdun in the ninth and tenth centuries was the center of a flourishing slave trade extending to Moslem Spain. Ganshof and André Dupont have proved that maritime relations remained unbroken between Italy and Provence from the eighth to the tenth century, the very period when Arab supremacy in the western Mediterranean was at its height, when the Arabs controlled Sicily and the other islands, and when the evidence speaks most frequently of their fleets, their piracy, and their raids upon the southern shores of Europe.

To supplement the interpretation of Merovingian and Carolingian economies by historians working with western evidence, Arabists such as Daniel C. Dennet have tried to assess the consequences of the Arab conquests from study of the Arab evidence. Failing to discover any reasons for the

40. Pirenne, *Mohammed and Charlemagne*, p. 246.
41. Lopez, "Mohammed and Charlemagne: A Revision," *Speculum*, XVIII (1943), 33.

Arabs to upset Mediterranean trade or to refuse to trade with
the West, Dennet concluded that international trade on the
Mediterranean was not ended by the Arabs. It was, in fact, to
their interest to continue trade with the West; they needed
the raw materials and slaves from Europe which they paid
for with their finished products. That political and military
competition or that religious differences would erect a barrier
between the western Christian and Moslem worlds seems in-
credible to Dennet. He believes rather that the Arab conquests
served to stimulate the western economy, a suggestion that is
supported by the research of various numismatists.

Other scholars are more uncertain about the immediate
impact of Arab power in the Mediterranean. Arabist Bernard
Lewis, for example, sees an initial break in trade because of
the hostilities, disruptions, and mutual distrust, but argues that
with their moderation, trade relations resumed in the eleventh
century. In the same vein, the Byzantinist S. A. Runciman has
observed that Byzantium resumed trade with the Arabs as
soon as the memory of Arab conquest and Byzantine-Arab
naval conflict diminished. In this context the interpretation of
A. R. Lewis is pertinent. Arguing first that the Arab domination of the Mediterranean was never as complete as Pirenne
thought, Lewis attempts to prove that Byzantium still controlled the eastern Mediterranean and was thus able to imple-
ment an economic policy aimed at a monopoly over trade with
the Arab lands as well as with Italy where she still had some
possessions. The West was therefore forced to obtain eastern
goods almost exclusively through such favored Italian ports as
Venice, Amalfi, and Bari, and even then such trade was seriously limited because Byzantium did not favor trade that
drained gold reserves outside her "monetary zone" located in
the eastern Mediterranean. This, according to Lewis, explains
why the flow of eastern goods to the West was reduced to a
trickle, why Pirenne found so few eastern products in the
West during the Carolingian period. What Lewis ignores is
why Byzantine economic policy changed so dramatically after
the Arabs ringed the Mediterranean. Perhaps the new pattern
of trade with Arab dominated lands forced Byzantium to extreme monetary precautions so as not to exhaust her gold
resources, but if this is true, it indicates that the Arabs did
indeed upset Mediterranean trade. If they did not actually

halt East-West trade, they certainly reoriented it so as to deprive the West of most eastern goods and to force it increasingly to live off the resources of land. This explanation is reinforced by P. C. Roberts who has recently written that the "effect of the Islamic encirclement of the Mediterranean was on the *orientation* of trade." Beginning in the eighth century while the economic movement of the western Mediterranean was directed toward Baghdad, that of the Carolingian lands turned inward, toward regionalization, toward the north. Roberts concluded that the Arab conquests "ended forever the orientation of Gaulish trade toward the Empire." [42]

These conclusions which suggest that Pirenne may have been treading upon thin ice in ascribing the breakup of the traditional Mediterranean economy to the Arabs are partially neutralized by others bolstering his position. Verlinden seems ambivalent about the Carolingian economy. In his study of Verdun he found an intensive slave trade, but in a study of economic conditions in Carolingian Alsace, not far from Verdun, he sees no evidence of a "particularly strong economic life." From an impressive study of Carolingian records concerned with trade and urban life in the early Middle Ages, Fernand Vercauteren is convinced that the Arabs made "a barrier" of the Mediterranean, that after their arrival true urban centers no longer existed in the lands between the Loire and the Rhine. Henri Laurent searched in vain for a class of professional merchants in the Carolingian period. Ganshof found such a class, but not until the second half of the tenth century when, as Pirenne had emphasized, there was a definite upswing in the western economy. A classic study by Hans Van Werveke depicts trade even in natural produce as so rare and difficult that all large abbeys in the north sought to obtain lands with a wide geographical distribution in order to produce wine and other foodstuffs. These ecclesiastical establishments became almost self-sufficient. F.-J. Himly, who firmly believes that trade in the Carolingian period was rare, points out very pertinently that scattered references to papyri, silks, and spices, and reference to an elephant sent as a gift to Charlemagne by the caliph Harun al-Raschid, or to Charlemagne's response with a fine piece of woolen cloth from Flanders scarcely constitute sufficient evidence to argue for regular

42. Roberts, *Classica et Mediaevalia*, XXV (1964), 312.

international and regional trade. Of the same opinion after a
careful study of trade in the early Middle Ages, Philip Grierson declares: "All that we know of the social conditions of the
time suggests that the alternatives to trade were more important than trade itself: the *onus probandi* rests on those who
believe the contrary to have been the case." [43]

NUMISMATIC EVIDENCE

Since it is evident that the arguments for and
against regular East-West trade, routine regional trade, and
the existence of a class of professional merchants are inconclusive, it is all the more unfortunate that numismatists who
have interpreted the hoards of buried coins have little advanced a settlement of the problem. Arguing somewhat like
Dennet, Maurice Lombard finds what he calls an Islamic economic supremacy around the Mediterranean between the
seventh and eleventh centuries, a supremacy that stimulated
and developed the Mediterranean economy which had been
until then in serious decline. Responsible for this stimulation
were the vast quantities of crude gold in Persia and the gold
mines in Africa and eastern Asia that the Arabs had acquired
through conquest and had immediately put to use, striking
coins and placing them in circulation in the caliphate and ad-
joining lands. Needing slaves, wood, furs, and other raw
materials, the Arabs poured their gold dinars, known in Europe as the *mancus,* into the West, an action that contributed
to the economic revival of the eleventh century. Instead of
suffocating the western economy, the Arabs resuscitated it
with their gold and more highly developed economic methods.
The western medieval economy shows, therefore, slow pro-
gression from an underdeveloped one in the early Middle
Ages to one more highly developed in the High Middle Ages,
one that was gradually overtaking the economies of the Arab
and Byzantine lands. The Age of the Crusades may well
symbolize the emergence of the western economy and its

43. Grierson, "Commerce in the Dark Ages: A Critique of the
Evidence," *Transactions of the Royal Historical Society,* IX (1950), 140.

spectacular development during the twelfth and thirteenth centuries.

Supporting Lombard's interpretation, the numismatist Sture Bolin makes an ingenious attempt to establish a correlation between the fluctuation in value of the Carolingian silver penny and the Arab coins. When the Arabs acquired large quantities of silver in the Hindu Kush about 850, the value of silver fell so much in relation to that of gold that at this point, Bolin claims, the silver content of the Carolingian penny was increased in order to maintain its relative value. Later, when the Arabs acquired ample quantities of gold in Nubia, the value of silver then rose and the amount of silver in the Carolingian penny was accordingly reduced. But why should the Carolingians have made these changes in their penny? Because, Bolin argues, economic relations existed between the Arab and Carolingian worlds, making such changes necessary. He then traces the trade links between the East and the West, especially those between the Arab lands and the Scandinavian region. The hoards of Arab coins found along these routes convinced Bolin that there was trade, especially along a route running from Arab lands to Constantinople and then north to Scandinavia, an exchange point from where eastern products circulated west on the Baltic and North seas and from where the raw products of the West were taken to Arab and Byzantine markets.

Other numismatists have clouded the picture with still different interpretations of early medieval monetary history. Some support the thesis of Marc Bloch that from the late Roman imperial period there was an adverse commercial balance which lasted for centuries and resulted in a hemorrhage of gold from West to East. By the Carolingian period the West was virtually drained of her gold and it did not flow back until the resurgence of the western economy in the eleventh century. While not responsible for this hemorrhage, the Arabs certainly did not stem it and therefore indirectly hastened the decision of Charlemagne to mint only the silver penny. H. L. Adelson has suggested that around 650 the Arabs cut Byzantium off from her supply of gold and, impoverished, she was forced to reduce or abolish the purchase of raw materials from the West, causing serious economic decline under the Carolingians. If this suggestion is true, the Arabs were

ultimately responsible for the economic misfortunes of the
West.

In a study that complements his earlier one on trade, Grierson has interpreted the numismatic evidence quite differently
from Lombard and Bolin. There is not enough evidence, he
argues, to prove that the coin known as the *mancus* in western
Europe was an Arab coin. He contends that it was not and
concludes that "the importation of Arab gold in substantial
quantities into western Europe in the Dark Ages must therefore be regarded as non-proven." [44] The implication is obvious: commercial relations between the Arabs and the West
must have been minimal or non-existent. In another article he
relates the deficiency of gold in the West to the monetary
reforms in the late seventh century of the Arab caliph 'Abd
al-Malik and Hajjāj, his governor of Syria, that resulted in a
new gold dinar and a new silver dirham in the ratio of fourteen dirhams to one dinar. He sees repercussions of this reform in both the Byzantine Empire and the West. In the
Byzantine Empire it appears to have brought abandonment
of the new silver hexagrams that had been in circulation since
the emperor Heraclius and that had a ratio of eighteen silver
hexagrams to one gold shilling. In the West the Germanic
kingdoms ceased to coin the gold shilling which they had
taken over from the Roman Empire and, instead, began to
strike silver pennies at the rate of twelve pennies to one shilling. About the year 700, then, there were three mint ratios:
eighteen to one in the Byzantine Empire, fourteen to one in
Arab lands, and twelve to one in the West. These differences
in ratios, Grierson argues, affected the flow of money. The
Moslem world found it advantageous to export gold to Byzantium and to buy silver hexagrams that were converted into
silver dirhams. Legislation in Byzantium favored the importation of gold so that one finds there an abundance of gold coins
and a scarcity of silver. For the West, it was more profitable
to sell silver and buy gold, a circumstance that may partly
account for the rarity of gold coins and the establishment of
silver monometallism that lasted for five centuries. By drain-
ing the West of its remaining gold, the Arabs forced it over
to a silver coinage. If Grierson is correct, the Arabs did in-

44. Grierson, "Carolingian Europe and the Arabs: The Myth of the
Mancus," *Revue Belge de Philologie et d'Histoire,* XXXII (1954), 1074.

deed have considerable influence on the western economy.

Other scholars have also attacked the Lombard-Bolin position. The dearth of Arab gold coins in western Europe definitely indicates, according to Edouard Perroy, that Arab coinage did not circulate in the West. Calling the Lombard-Bolin position a mirage, Himly has categorically stated that he could find no numismatic evidence of extensive trade between the Carolingian and Arab lands, but of only a small luxury trade that had no impact upon the Carolingian economy. He is therefore certain that Carolingian trade was mostly self-contained and that the minimal external trade relations were in the north with Anglo-Saxon England and with the Varangians.

In an evaluation of numismatic evidence relating to the Carolingian economy, K. F. Morrison warns the economic historian to use it with extreme caution because it tells him nothing certain about trade routes or about the volume of trade. With his position clear, he then emphasizes that there is "no numismatic evidence of extensive contact with peoples outside the Carolingian empire" and that written sources support this conclusion.[45] The implication is that numismatic studies of the Carolingian period, like those on trade, are inconclusive.

TENTH CENTURY

Contrary to most historians who have concentrated their fire on that portion of Pirenne's theory concerned with the period between the late Roman Empire and Charlemagne, some have criticized his treatment of the ninth and tenth centuries. These historians are obviously under the influence of Dopsch and, whether or not they agree with him on the continuity of Roman institutions, they accept his thesis that the Carolingian renaissance was economic as well as intellectual and that it contributed to a gradual economic improvement during the tenth century that inaugurated the dramatic re-

45. Morrison, "Numismatics and Carolingian Trade: A Critique of the Evidence," *Speculum*, XXXVIII (1963), 432. See also Morrison, *Carolingian Coinage*.

vival of the eleventh. From evidence relating to trade, agriculture, and demography they found enough economic activity in the ninth and tenth centuries to convince them that it was a kind of "take-off period" for the rapid economic progress of the following century. Guillaume Des Marez, Latouche, Renée Doehaerd, and J. Lestocquoy, among others, believed that the domanial economy of the Carolingians provided a surplus of goods and that this condition explains the rise of markets and fairs, the development of regional and interregional trade between towns, castles, abbeys, and other strategic points, and the appearance of merchants who can be found purveying the goods. Des Marez ascribed a surplus of crops that stimulated trade and urban life to more intensive cultivation of lands on the great estates and to the conversion of forests and wasteland into arable land. Renée Doehaerd has characterized economic expansion in these centuries as a "continuous phenomenon." Latouche regarded the healthy agrarian economy of northern Europe as the foundation of the future economic advances. Lopez has spoken of the renaissance of the tenth century. David Herlihy has described an agricultural revolution in Italy and southern France which he thinks may well have been "a necessary preliminary for the urban revolution." [46]

In a study of medieval technology and its influence on social change, Lynn White has rendered perhaps the most harsh criticism of Pirenne's theory. He grants that Pirenne called attention to the shift in focus of Europe from south to north, but states that historians "have now destroyed Pirenne's thesis in the greatest detail." "Mediterranean commerce," he writes, "suffered a long and steady decline; the Islamic conquest did not close the Mediterranean to the meagre trade still existing between the Orient and the West; economic historians can draw no sharp line between Merovingian and Carolingian times as regards contacts with the East." If the explanation of Pirenne does not account for the movement of activity northward away from the Mediterranean, what does? White's answer is agricultural revolution. "By the early ninth century all the major interlocking elements of this revolution had been developed: the heavy plough, the open fields, the

46. Herlihy, "The Agrarian Revolution in Southern France and Italy, 801–1150," *Speculum,* XXXIII (1958), 37.

modern harness, the triennial rotation . . ."[47] This revolution produced the surplus food considered by other historians as the element responsible for an upward economic turn and as the fuel for the subsequent economic revival.

Carlo Cipolla feels that Pirenne and his critics have generalized too much from too little data. To the eyes of an economist there was very little economic activity between the fifth and eleventh century. Cipolla rightly observes that there was no investment of capital in instruments of production, that production of goods was low, that consumption was limited, that communications were hazardous and irregular, that monetary circulation was weak, and that the balance of trade with the East was so unfavorable as to cause a chronic deficit and a descending demographic curve. These observations lend credence to the conclusion that in the long period up to the eleventh century the economy was inactive or severely depressed, that from the political disintegration of the Roman Empire in the West to the Carolingian period there was steady decline accelerated by the Arab conquests around the Mediterranean. Sharing this belief, Marc Bloch, R. H. C. Davis, Robert Boutruche, and Léopold Genicot agree that the period between the fourth and eighth centuries saw the end of one world and the genesis of another.

PIRENNE'S THESIS TODAY

What, then, can be said for the Pirenne theory? Much of the subsequent research has weakened his thesis. He obviously overemphasized Merovingian economic activity and its continuity with the Roman, and may have underemphasized Carolingian economic activity. He seems also to have assigned to the Arabs too decisive a role in the destruction of Mediterranean economic unity and, consequently, in the emergence of the Middle Ages. His treatment of politics and institutions is victim to the same weaknesses as his interpretation of economic and social history—overemphasis regarding the continuity of Roman institutions in the German kingdoms and some delusion in believing that the German chiefs took

47. White, *Medieval Technology and Social Change*, pp. 77–78.

the Roman emperors as models. Although correct in stressing the exclusively secular bases of German political authority prior to Charlemagne and his father Pepin, Pirenne perhaps attributed too much to the spiritual sanction of secular authority given by the church. It is true that his bent toward social and economic causation caused him to slight the cultural and religious differences separating the ancient from the medieval world or to place such differences out of focus as in distorting Theodoric's love of classical culture and his patronage of such as Boethius and Cassiodorus. Undoubtedly there was more religious and educational reform and more cultural achievement in the so-called Carolingian renaissance than Pirenne admits, but not in the inflated proportion that many historians would have it. Like most theories concerned with the explanation of vast historical transformations, Pirenne's suffers from over and understatement, generalizes at times upon evidence too scant and cryptic, and explicates too much from certain types of evidence. Later research suggests that the Carolingian and post-Carolingian periods were not as dark socially and economically as Pirenne portrayed, that in the ninth and tenth centuries there were important economic and technological developments from which emerged in the eleventh century such economic phenomena as the town, international trade, and the middle class of merchants and artisans, all of which Pirenne allegedly regarded as springing up rapidly without antecedents.

But Pirenne's theory has by no means been completely discredited. His grand tableau of the early Middle Ages has actually been little changed. It is not wholly accurate to say that he had western Europe leaping into economic revival in the eleventh century without any period of preparation. He traces the momentum for the revival back to the late ninth and tenth centuries which he clearly identified as a preparatory period. From the middle of the tenth century he discerned a rise in population; increased cultivation resulting from the clearance of forests and the reclamation of land from swamps, moors, and coastal waters; a growing political stability essential for economic activity; and a surge in trade along the waterways and overland routes converging on such points as Venice and Flanders. For Pirenne these were the roots of the economic flowering in the eleventh century.

Scholars continue to under and overemphasize the cultural vigor of the Merovingian and Carolingian periods and to distort Christian influence on pagan thought. Some see St. Augustine imbibing in classical thought. Others see him at its fringes, sabotaging it and preparing the way for a completely new view of man and his use of knowledge. Some see Pope Gregory the Great as a competent continuator of good Latin and an admirer of the classical tradition. Others point to his simple Latin compositions, seeing him as epitomizing the difference between sophisticated, rational, classical thought and simple, mystical, Christian thought. These scholars in cultural and religious history with their subjective evaluations will continue to agree or disagree with Pirenne.

Dawson's conclusions, however, parallel those of Pirenne. Like Pirenne, he interpreted Charlemagne's coronation as symbolizing the beginning of the Middle Ages. Pierre Riché's recent study of education and culture in the barbarian West has confirmed the main lines of Pirenne's interpretation of the cultural and religious transition from the ancient to the medieval world. Like Pirenne, Riché sees a transformation in education and thought during the late imperial period that was even given impetus with the advent of the Germans. In spite of the decline of classical culture and its conversion to serve Christian truth, Riché believes that the aristocratic contemporaries of the Merovingians Chilperic and Dagobert still lived in an antique atmosphere, that Merovingian Gaul remained a part of the Mediterranean cultural community into the first half of the seventh century, and that not until the second half of that century did cultured men become scarce and barbarism sweep over the West. By Charlemagne's time Roman education and thought were dead in western Europe.

Some historians have found Pirenne deficient in his analysis of the evidence but most, except perhaps classical historians, admit that his large picture or synthesis has credibility. He was, after all, not the first historian to perceive that after the empire in the West no longer existed politically some features of its civilization continued. He did not deny that during the third and fourth centuries political disintegration, social and economic misfortunes, cultural malaise, and a profound shift in religious values occurred, but he did not believe that they alone ended Graeco-Roman civilization. Despite the

German conquests with their turmoil and new political ar-
rangements, no new civilization arose because the Germans
were generally willing to partake of the Mediterranean civilization and the unity upon which it depended. What im-
pressed Pirenne was how much all this had changed in the
West by the time of the Carolingians. He noticed that after
600 Italy lay prostrate with the Ostrogothic kingdom destroyed by Justinian's unfortunate attempt to reconquer the
West; that all the lands ringing the Mediterranean, except
for some in southern Europe, were under Arab dominion; and
that the Carolingian state was oriented northward rather than
southward to the Mediterranean, its center lying between the
Loire and the Rhine. He sensed also that there was much less
trade, especially on the Mediterranean between the West and
the East, that few real towns still existed, that the economy
was much more agrarian, and that culturally, Europe was
relatively barren. But why had such change come after 600?
For Pirenne the logical reason was the Arab conquest of the
Mediterranean, which made it a barrier rather than a boulevard for East-West exchanges, causing the orbit of power in
the East to shift to Baghdad and in the West, to the north.
This transformation isolated western Europe and presaged
seignorialism, feudalism, and the domination of the church,
all of which were consecrated by the coronation of Charlemagne in 800.

Although giving the Arabs too decisive a part in this
change, Pirenne was the first to understand that they had
exercised a profound influence upon the Mediterranean and
the West. In comparing the culture of the Arab lands with that
of the West, he saw an impoverished and underdeveloped
West facing in the East a thriving, creative culture rooted in
a money economy. This picture was little changed until the
West revived and pushed its way back into the Mediterranean
during the eleventh century, a push climaxed by the First
Crusade. For the first time in centuries the West again traded
on the Mediterranean and established regular contacts with
the East. Without this development the extraordinary achievements of the twelfth and thirteenth centuries would have been
inconceivable. One may fault Pirenne for his details, but in
terms of western history his synthesis is both credible and
imaginative. Its hypotheses account for the relative darkness

of the early Middle Ages and for the recovery and vigorous achievements of western Europe in the High Middle Ages. By placing in proper perspective those centuries between 400 and 1000 that had been ignored by classical historians and slighted by medievalists, Pirenne dramatically reminded historians that in this period lie the answers to the uniqueness of western history. Historiographically he did even more. He delivered medievalists from Gibbon's spell by forcing them to acknowledge that they must repudiate much of what Gibbon had argued, and that this meant reexamination of a historiographical tradition dating back to the Renaissance. For this reason alone Pirenne's *Mahomet et Charlemagne* ranks among the historical classics. It compels every student of the Middle Ages to wrestle with its concepts because within their framework rests a truer understanding and appreciation of the Middle Ages.

It may well be that what Gibbon referred to as the world's great debate will never end because we lack the evidence for a real solution. For the whole period from the third to the ninth century there are gaps and uncertainties. To lessen these gaps and to remove some uncertainties further research by Arabists and Byzantinists is definitely needed. Too much of the research so far has been done by specialists in western history using the evidence of western Europe and viewing the problem through western eyes. For a truer perspective there must be greater focus on Arab and Byzantine evidence. But even with further research by Byzantinists and Arabists and assistance from the classical and medieval archaeologist, the numismatist, and the art historian, some of the fundamental questions will never be resolved. What new evidence and insights emerge will little alter our present understanding. The large gaps in our knowledge can never be appreciably narrowed. Each historian working on this problem will need to use his historical imagination to recreate what happened, to suggest the known for the unknown, and to assemble the meager facts in proper perspective.

Did Pirenne, knowing what he did about the evidence, think that he had resolved the great debate? He himself has answered this question. Although he had no philosophy of history and rarely wrote about method, he clearly expressed his view of the historian's task. The historian must grasp all

that he can of the concrete with the realization that he can
never directly observe past events. He must then relate these
concrete facts to collective phenomena if he would attain his
highest objective—the study of the development of human
societies in space and time. For each historian, criticism and
proper appreciation of evidence is an essential first step that
must lead always to asking whether the conclusions drawn
from the evidence meet the standards of credibility. If he is
satisfied that his analysis of the sources is credible, he should
then advance to historical narrative which must combine synthesis and hypothesis. The proper end of all research is historical synthesis, but it cannot stand alone; it must be
animated and given its *raison d'être* by hypothesis. History,
therefore, is a conjectural or a subjective discipline. It has to
be, not only because of what each historian brings to it, but because it contains the element of chance. Finally, the historian
must realize that a synthesis incorporating these qualities and
allowing for human deficiencies will ever be unfulfilled unless
it is comparative. Only by comparision of events, institutions,
societies, and civilizations can the historian achieve a balanced
perspective.

Elaborating upon this view of the historian's task, Pirenne
stated on one occasion: "All those engaged in searching for the
truth understand that the glimpses they have of it are necessarily fleeting. They glow for an instant and then make way
for new and always more dazzling brightness. Quite different
from that of the artist, the work of the scholar is inevitably
provisional. He knows this and rejoices in it because the rapid
obsoleteness of his books is the very proof of the progress of
his field of knowledge." [48] And, again, upon completion of the
final volume of his *Histoire de Belgique,* he wrote: "If it is
true that every attempt at a synthesis is necessarily provisional, it is also true that by the hypotheses it proposes, the
connections it establishes, and the problems it poses, it is able
to assist in scientific progress. There is only a science of the
general and this is true of history as for the other fields of
knowledge. To call upon a historian to delay his construction
until all the material of his subject has been assembled and

48. From a speech given on 12 May 1912 and printed in *Manifesta-
tion en l'honneur de M. le Professeur Henri Pirenne* (Mons, 1912), pp.
57–58.

all the questions involved elucidated, is to condemn him to a perpetual waiting, because the materials will never be completely known, nor the questions definitively resolved, because as a field of knowledge develops it is always uncovering new problems. What should be demanded of an author is that he utilize all the resources at his disposal at the moment he writes." [49]

When he wrote *Mahomet et Charlemagne,* Pirenne met these demands. He was under no illusion that he was in command of all the evidence or that what he wrote would completely resolve the centuries-old debate, but he knew that he brought to the problem a different perspective which he hoped would bring new understanding and inspire historians to reexamine it. He would probably be disappointed in learning that his theory has generally been ignored by classical historians who continue blithely along, serene in their faith that most of what Gibbon told them is the truth, that they need have no concern for what happened after 330, 395, 410, 455, or 476 because this was when the ancient world ended, but that he failed to convince all his peers, that his facts have been corrected, or that his theory has been revised, would not distress but delight him because it would be a measure of how much his work had advanced our knowledge of western civilization. And yet Pirenne's theory, though revised, has not yet been replaced by any other more credible or convincing on the enigma of the end of the ancient world and the beginning of the Middle Ages.

49. Pirenne, *Histoire de Belgique,* VII, xi–xii.

Bibliography

The **boldface** *numbers following entries indicate pages on which the author or the work is mentioned in the text.*

* Books in paperback editions are marked with an asterisk.

Adelson, H. L., *Light Weight Solidi and Byzantine Trade During the Sixth and Seventh Centuries* (New York, 1957). **77**
———, "Early Medieval Trade Routes," *American Historical Review,* LXV (1960), 271–287.
Altheim, F., *Le déclin du monde antique. Examen des causes de la décadence* (Paris, 1953).
Amyot, J., *Les vies des hommes illustres . . . par Plutarque de Chaeronée translate de Grec en Français* (Paris, 1582), vol. I. **19**
Aubin, H., "Die Frage nach der Scheide zwischen Altertum und Mittelalter," *Historische Zeitschrift,* CLXXII (1951), 245–263. **64**
*Augustine, *City of God,* in *The Writings of the Fathers of the Church)* (Washington, D.C., 1950–1954), vols. VI–VIII. See the abridged edition in paperback with foreword by V. J. Bourke (New York, Doubleday Image, 1958). **7, 14, 15, 18, 35, 83**
*Bark, W. C., *Origins of the Medieval World* (New York, Doubleday Anchor, 1960). **67**
Baynes, N. H., "The Decline of the Roman Power in Western Europe. Some Modern Explanations," *Journal of Roman Studies,* XXXIII (1943), 29–35. **52, 53, 54, 70**
———, "M. Pirenne and the Unity of the Mediterranean World," *Journal of Roman Studies,* XVIII (1929), 224–235.
Beer, G. de, *Gibbon and His World* (London, 1968).
Beloch, K. J., *Die Bevölkerung der griechisch-römischen Welt* (Leipzig, 1886). **38, 46**
———, "Die Bevölkerung Italiens im Altertum," *Klio,* III (1903), 471–490.
———, "Der Verfall der antiken Kultur," *Historische Zeitschrift,* LXXXIV (1900), 1–38.
Bèze, T. de, *Histoire ecclésiastique des Eglises Réformées au royaume de France,* new ed. (Paris, 1883–1889), 3 vols. **20**
Biondo, *Historiarum ab Inclinatione Romanorum Imperii Decades,* ed. Froben (Basel, 1531). **17, 18**
Bloch, M., "Le problème de l'or au moyen âge," *Les Annales d'Histoire Sociale,* V (1933), 1–34. See the English translation in M. Bloch, *Land and Work in Mediaeval Europe* (Berkeley, 1967), pp. 186–229. **53, 77, 81**
———, "La dernière oeuvre d'Henri Pirenne," *Les Annales d'Histoire Sociale,* X (1938), 325–330.
———, *Esquisse d'une histoire monétaire de l'Europe* (Paris, 1954).
Boak, A. E. R., *Manpower Shortage and the Fall of the Roman Empire in the West* (Ann Arbor, 1955). **37, 38, 44**
Bolin, S., "Mohammed, Charlemagne and Ruric," *Scandinavian Economic History Review,* I (1953), 5–39. **77, 78, 79**
Boutruche, R., *Seigneurie et féodalité* (Paris, 1959). **81**
Boyce, G. C., "The Legacy of Henri Pirenne," *Byzantion,* XV (1940–41), 449–464.
Bratianu, G. I., *Etudes byzantines d'histoire économique et sociale* (Paris, 1938). **65, 66**

Bruni, *Historiarum Florentini Populi Libri XII,* in L. A. Muratori, *Rerum Italicarum Scriptores,* vol. XIX. See also new ed. by E. Santini (Città di Castello, 1914). **17**

Brutzkus, J., "Trade with Eastern Europe, 800–1200," *Economic History Review,* XIII (1943), 31–41. **71**

Bücher, K., *Etudes d'histoire et d'économie politique* (Brussels, 1901). **49**

———, *Die Entstehung der Volkswirtschaft,* 6th ed. (Tübingen, 1920–1921), 2 vols. See the English translation by S. M. Wickett, *Industrial Evolution* (New York, 1901).

*Burckhardt, J., *The Age of Constantine* (New York, 1949). **26**

Burns, C. D., *The First Europe: A Study of the Establishment of Medieval Christendom, A.D. 400–800* (London, 1947). **66**

Burr, G. L., "How the Middle Ages Got Their Name," *American Historical Review,* XX (1915), 813–815.

Bury, J. B., *History of the Later Roman Empire, 395–565* (London, 1923), 2 vols. **55**

———, "Causes of the Survival of the Roman Empire in the East," in *Selected Essays,* ed. H. Temperley (Cambridge, 1930).

Cantor, N. F., *Medieval History: The Life and Death of a Civilization* (New York, 1963), p. 31.

Cary, M., *A History of Rome Down to the Reign of Constantine,* 2nd ed. (London, 1950), pp. 773–776.

Cellarius, *Nucleus Historiae Inter Antiquam et Novam Mediae* (1675). Later, in 1688, Cellarius wrote a *History of the Middle Ages from the Times of Constantine the Great to the Capture of Constantinople by the Turks.* **21**

*Chabod, F., *Machiavelli and the Renaissance* (New York, Harper Torchbook, 1965).

Chamberlain, H. S., *Die Grundlagen des neunzehten Jahrhunderts,* 12th ed. (Munich, 1918), 2 vols. **28, 29, 33**

Cipolla, C., "Encore Mahomet et Charlemagne. L'économie politique au secours de l'histoire," *Les Annales d'Histoire Sociale,* IV (1949), **81**

Condorcet, *Esquisse d'un tableau historique des progrès de l'esprit humain,* new ed. (Paris, 1933). An English translation was published at London in 1795. **23**

Cortese, *Dialogus de Hominibus Doctis,* in F. Villani, *Liber de Civitatis Florentiae Famosis Civibus,* ed. G. C. Galletti (Florence, 1847). **18**

Coulanges, Fustel de, *Histoire des institutions politiques de l'ancienne France* (Paris, 1888–1892), 6 vols. **57, 58, 63**

———, *L'invasion germanique et la fin de l'Empire* (Paris, 1891).

Dante, *De Monarchia,* trans. F. J. Church (London, 1879).

Davis, R. H. C., *A History of Medieval Europe from Constantine to Saint Louis* (London, 1957). **81**

Dawson, C., "Edward Gibbon," *Proceedings of the British Academy,* XX (1934), 162–174. **57, 66, 67, 83**

*———, *The Making of Europe: An Introduction to the History of European Unity* (New York, Meridian, 1956).

Demougeot, E., *De l'unité à la division de l'Empire Romain, 395–410. Essai sur le gouvernement impérial* (Paris, 1951). **64**

Dennet, D. C., Jr., "Pirenne and Muhammad," *Speculum,* XXIII (1948), 165–190. **73, 74, 76**

Des Marez, G., "On demande une étude sur les *civitates* de la Belgique seconde," *Bulletin de la Classe des Lettres de l'Académie Royale de Belgique,* XV (1929), 71–91. **80**

*Dill, S., *Roman Society in the Last Century of the Western Empire* (New York, Meridian, 1958). **45**

Doehaerd, R., *L'expansion économique belge au moyen âge* (Brussels, 1946).   **68, 80**

Dopsch, A., *The Economic and Social Foundations of European Civilization* (London, 1937). This is a translation and abridgement of *Wirtschaftliche und soziale Grundlagen der Europäischen Kulturgeschichte*, 2nd ed. (Vienna, 1923–1924).   **57, 63, 67, 68, 69, 71**

Dupont, A., *Les relations commerciales entre les cités maritimes du Languedoc et les cités méditerranéennes d'Espagne et d'Italie du Xe au XIIe siècle* (Nîmes, 1942).   **71, 73**

Erasmus, *Antibarbarorum Liber*, new ed. in A. Hyma, *The Youth of Erasmus* (Ann Arbor, 1930).   **19**

*Erikson, E. H., *Young Man Luther* (New York, Norton, 1958).   **47**

Ferguson, W. F., *The Renaissance in Historical Thought* (Boston, 1948).

Ferrero, G., *The Ruin of Ancient Civilization and the Triumph of Christianity* (New York, 1921).   **42**

Finley, M. I., "Arthur E. R. Boak, Manpower Shortage and the Fall of the Roman Empire in the West," *Journal of Roman Studies*, XLVIII (1958), 156–164.

Frank, T., "Race Mixture in the Roman Empire," *American Historical Review*, XXI (1916), 689–708.   **34**

*Ganshof, F. L., *Frankish Institutions Under Charlemagne* (New York, Norton, 1970).   **68, 73, 75**

——, "Notes sur les ports de Provence du VIIIe au Xe siècle," *Revue Historique*, CLXXXIII (1938), 28–37.

——, "Pirenne (Henri)," in *Biographie Nationale publiée par l'Académie Royale des Sciences, des Lettres et des Beaux-Arts*, XXX (1959), cols. 671–723.

Genicot, L., *Contours of the Middle Ages* (London, 1967).   **81**

Gibbon, Edward, *The History of the Decline and Fall of the Roman Empire*, ed. J. B. Bury (London, 1896–1900). There are other editions, some of which are abridged and in paperback.   **7, 10, 11, 23, 25, 26, 27, 30, 35, 46, 48, 50, 56, 57, 59, 61, 65, 69, 85, 87**

——, *Memoirs of My Life*, ed. G. A. Bonnard (London, 1966).

Gilliam, J. F., "The Plague under Marcus Aurelius," *American Journal of Philology*, LXXXII (1961), 225–251.

Gobineau, J. A. de, *Essai sur l'inégalité des races humaines*, 2nd ed. (Paris, 1884), 2 vols. See the English translation by A. Collins, *The Inequality of Human Races* (New York, 1915).   **28, 29, 31, 33**

Grierson, P., "Carolingian Europe and the Arabs: The Myth of the Mancus," *Revue Belge de Philologie et d'Histoire*, XXXII (1954), 1059–1074.   **76, 78**

——, "Commerce in the Dark Ages: A Critique of the Evidence," *Transactions of the Royal Historical Society*, IX (1959), 123–140.

——, "The Monetary Reforms of 'Abd al-Malik. Their Metrological Basis and Their Financial Repercussions," *Journal of Economic and Social History of the Orient*, III (1960), 241–264.

Halphen, L., *Les barbares des grandes invasions aux conquêtes turques du XIe siècle*, 3rd ed. (Paris, 1936).   **64**

*Haywood, R. M., *The Myth of Rome's Fall* (New York, Apollo, 1958).   **55**

Heichelheim, F. M., *Wirtschaftsgeschichte des Altertums* (Leiden, 1938), 2 vols.   **51**

Heitland, W. E., *Iterum, or a Further Discussion of the Roman Fate* (Cambridge, 1925).   **42**

——, *The Roman Fate* (Cambridge, 1922).

——, *The Last Words on the Roman Municipalities* (Cambridge, 1928).

Herlihy, D., "The Agrarian Revolution in Southern France and Italy, 801–1150," *Speculum*, XXXIII (1958), 23–41.   **80**

*Herodotus, *The Histories*, trans. A. de Sélincourt (Harmondsworth, Penguin, 1960). **9**

Hillgarth, J. N., "Visigothic Spain and Early Christian Ireland," *Proceedings of the Royal Irish Academy*, LXII (1962), 167–194.

Himly, F.-J., "Y a-t-il emprise musulmane sur l'économie des états européens du VIIIe au Xe siècle?" *Schweizerische Zeitschrift für Geschichte*, V (1955), 31–81. **75, 79**

Homo, L., *La civilisation romaine* (Paris, 1930). **44**

Huntington, E., "Changes of Climate and History," *American Historical Review*, XVIII (1913), 213–232. **38, 39**

———, *The Pulse of Asia, Civilization and Climate* (New Haven, 1915).

———, "Climatic Change and Agricultural Exhaustion as Elements in the Fall of Rome," *Quarterly Journal of Economics*, XXXI (1917), 173–208.

Jellema, D., "Frisian Trade in the Dark Ages," *Speculum*, XXX (1955), 15–36. **71**

Jones, A. H. M., *The Later Roman Empire 284–602. A Social, Economic and Administrative Survey* (Oxford, 1964), 3 vols. **44, 64, 65**

Jordan, D. P., "Gibbon's 'Age of Constantine' and the Fall of Rome," *History and Theory*, VIII (1969), 71–96.

Kaegi, W. E., Jr., *Byzantium and the Decline of Rome* (Princeton, 1968).

Katz, S., *The Jews in the Visigothic and Frankish Kingdoms of Spain and Gaul* (Cambridge, Mass., 1937). **71**

Kornemann, E., "Das Problem des Untergangs der antiken Welt," *Vergangenheit und Gegenwart*, XII (1922), 193–202, 241–254. **43**

Lambrechts, P., "Le commerce des Syriens en Gaule du haut empire à l'époque mérovingienne," *L'Antiquité Classique*, VI (1937), 35–61. **71**

Landry, A., "Quelques aperçus concernant la dépopulation dans l'antiquité gréco-romaine," *Revue Historique*, CLXXVII (1936), 1–33.

*Latouche, R., *The Birth of Western Economy: Economic Aspects of the Dark Ages* (New York, Harper Torchbook, 1966). **68, 69, 80**

Laurent, H., "Marchands du palais et marchands d'abbayes," *Revue Historique*, CLXXXIII (1938), 281–297. **71, 75**

———, "Les travaux de M. Pirenne sur la fin du monde antique et les débuts du moyen âge," *Byzantion*, VII (1932), 495–509.

Leopold, H. M. R., *De Spiegel van het verleden. Beschouwingen over den Ondergang van het Romeinsche Rijk naar Aanleiding van het huidige Wereldgebeuren* (Rotterdam, 1918). **51**

Lestocquoy, J. F., "The Tenth Century," *Economic History Review*, XVII (1947), 1–14. **80**

———, "De l'unité à la pluralité. Le paysage urbain en Gaule du Ve au IXe siècle," *Les Annales d'Histoire Sociale*, VIII (1953), 159–172.

Lewis, A. R., *Naval Power and Trade in the Mediterranean, A.D. 500–1100* (Princeton, 1951). **71, 74**

———, *The Northern Seas. Shipping and Commerce in Northern Europe, A.D. 300–1100* (Princeton, 1958).

*Lewis, B., *The Arabs in History* (London, Arrow Book, 1958). **74**

Liebig, J., *Chemie in ihrer Anwendung auf Agrikultur und Physiologie*, 9th ed. (Braunschweig, 1876). See the English translation by L. Playfair, *Organic Chemistry in Its Applications to Agriculture and Physiology* (Boston, 1841). **39, 40**

Lombard, M., "Les bases monétaires d'une suprématie économique. L'or musulman du VIIe au XIe siècle," *Les Annales d'Histoire Sociale*, II (1947), 143–160. **76, 77, 78, 79**

———, "Mahomet et Charlemagne. Le problème économique," *Les Annales d'Histoire Sociale*, II (1948), 188–199.

Lopez, R. S., "Le problème des relations Anglo-Byzantines du septième
    au dixième siècle," *Byzantion,* XVIII (1948), 139–162.   **71, 72, 73**
————, "Mohammed and Charlemagne: A Revision," *Speculum,* XVIII
    (1943), 14–38.
————, "East and West in the Early Middle Ages," *Relazioni del X
    Congresso Internazionale di Scienze Storiche,* III (1955), 129–137.
————, "Still Another Renaissance," *American Historical Review,* LVII
    (1955), 1–21.
————, "Of Towns and Trade," in *Life and Thought in the Early
    Middle Ages,* ed. R. S. Hoyt (Minneapolis, 1967), pp. 30–50.
*Lot, F., *The End of the Ancient World and the Beginnings of the
    Middle Ages* (New York, Harper Torchbook, 1961).   **35, 38, 47,
    51, 52, 63, 64**
Low, D. M., *Edward Gibbon* (London, 1937).
Loyn, H. R., *Anglo-Saxon England and the Norman Conquest* (London,
    1962).
Lyon, B., "L'oeuvre de Henri Pirenne après vingt-cinq ans," *Le Moyen
    Age,* LXVI (1960), 437–493.
*Machiavelli, *History of Florence and of the Affairs of Italy from the
    Earliest Times to the Death of Lorenzo the Magnificent* (New
    York, Harper Torchbook, 1960).   **7, 17, 18, 31**
Mazzarino, S., *The End of the Ancient World* (New York, 1966).
Melanchthon, *Declamatio de Corrigendis Adolescentiae Studiis, Opera
    Quae Supersunt Omnia,* ed. C. G. Brettschneider (Halle, 1834–
    1860).   **19**
Momigliano, A. (ed.), *The Conflict Between Paganism and Christianity
    in the Fourth Century* (Oxford, 1963).
Mommsen, T. E., "Petrarch's Conception of the 'Dark Ages,' " *Speculum,*
    XVII (1942), 226–242.
Montesquieu, *Considerations on the Causes of the Greatness of the
    Romans and Their Decline,* trans. D. Lowenthal (New York, 1965).
    7, 23, 24, 25
Morrison, K. F., "Numismatics and Carolingian Trade: A Critique of
    the Evidence," *Speculum,* XXXVIII (1963), 403–432.   **79**
————, *Carolingian Coinage* (New York, 1967).
*Moss, H. St. L. B., *The Birth of the Middle Ages* (Oxford, Galaxy
    Book, 1935).   **64**
————, "The Economic Consequences of the Barbarian Invasions," *Eco-
    nomic History Review,* VII (1937), 209–216.
Musset, L., *Les invasions: les vagues germaniques* (Paris, 1965).
Nauclerus, J., *Memorabilem Omnis Aetatis et Omnium Gentium Chronici
    Commentarii* (Cologne, 1544).   **19**
Nilsson, M. P., *Imperial Rome* (New York, 1926).   **33, 34, 35**
Oertel, F., in *Cambridge Ancient History* (Cambridge, 1934–1939),
    vols. X, XII.
Orosius, *Seven Books Against the Pagans,* trans. I. W. Raymond (New
    York, 1936).   **14, 15**
Otto, bishop of Freising, *The Two Cities: A Chronicle of Universal His-
    tory to the Year 1146 A.D.,* trans. C. C. Mierow (New York, 1928).
    16
Petrarch, *Apologia Contra Cuiusdam Anonymi Galli Calumnias,* in *Opera
    Omnia* (Basel, 1554).   **16, 17, 18**
————, *Epistolae de Rebus Familiaribus,* ed. J. Fracassetti (Florence,
    1859).
Perroy, E., "Encore Mahomet et Charlemagne," *Revue Historique,*
    CCXII (1954), 232–238.   **79**

Piganiol, A., *L'Empire chrétien (325–395)* (Paris, 1947).

Pirenne, H., *Souvenirs de captivité en Allemagne (mars 1916–novembre 1918)* (Brussels, 1921). **60**

———, "Mahomet et Charlemagne," *"Revue Belge de Philologie et d'Histoire,* I (1922), 77–86. **8, 61–87**

———, "Un contraste économique: Mérovingiens et Carolingiens," *Revue Belge de Philologie et d'Histoire,* II (1923), 223–235.

———, "La tâche de l'historien," *Le Flambeau,* XIV (1931), 5–22. For the English translation see S. A. Rice (ed.), *Methods in Social Science* (Chicago, 1931).

———, *Histoire de Belgique* (Brussels, 1932), vol. VII. **86**

*———, *A History of Europe from the End of the Roman World in the West to the Beginnings of the Western States* (New York, Doubleday Anchor, 1958), 2 vols. See also the French edition, *Histoire de l'Europe des invasions au XVIe siècle* (Brussels, 1936). **60**

*———, *Mohammed and Charlemagne* (New York, 1939). Paperback edition by Barnes and Noble (New York, 1955). **61–87**

Pirenne, J., "Henri Pirenne," *Le Flambeau,* XIX (1936), 513–554. **61**

Polybius, *History,* trans. W. R. Paton (London, 1922–1927), 6 vols. **9, 18, 31**

Riché, P., *Education et culture dans l'occident barbare, VIe–VIIIe siècles* (Paris, 1962). **83**

Riising, A., "The Fate of Henri Pirenne's Theses on the Consequences of the Islamic Expansion," *Classica et Mediaevalia,* XIII (1952), 87–130.

Roberts, P. C., "The Pirenne Thesis: Economies or Civilizations, Towards Reformulation," *Classica et Mediaevalia,* XXV (1964), 297–315. **65, 66, 75**

Robertson, W., *View of the Progress of Society in Europe from the Subversion of the Roman Empire to the Beginning of the Sixteenth Century,* in *Works* (London, 1840), vol. III. **23**

Rostovtzeff, M., *The Social and Economic History of the Roman Empire* (Oxford, 1926). **39, 44, 53, 54, 65, 70**

———, "The Decay of the Ancient World and Its Economic Explanations," *Economic History Review,* II (1930), 197–214.

* Runciman, S. A., *Byzantine Civilisation* (New York, Meridian, 1956). **74**

Sabbe, E., "L'importation des tissus orientaux en Europe occidentale au haut moyen âge," *Revue Belge de Philologie et d'Histoire,* XIV (1935), 811–848, 1260–1288. **72**

———, "Papyrus et parchemin au haut moyen âge," in *Miscellanea Historica in Honorem Leonis van der Essen* (Brussels, 1947), I, 95–103.

Salvioli, G., *Le capitalisme dans le monde antique* (Paris, 1906). **49**

Saunders, J. J., "The Debate on the Fall of Rome," *History,* XLVIII (1963), 1–17.

Seeck, O., *Geschichte des Untergangs der antiken Welt* (Stuttgart, 1910–1919), 6 vols. **34, 35**

Simkhovitch, V. G., "Rome's Fall Reconsidered," *Political Science Quarterly,* XXXI (1916), 201–243. **39**

———, *Towards the Understanding of Jesus* (New York, 1937).

Sorel, G., *La ruine du monde antique. Conception matérialiste de l'histoire,* 3rd ed. (Paris, 1933). **50**

Spengler, O., *Der Untergang des Abendlandes* (Munich, 1918–1922). See the English translation by C. F. Atkinson under the title *The Decline of the West* (London, 1926–1928), 2 vols. **31, 32, 33**

Stephenson, C., "The Problem of the Common Man in Early Mediaeval

Europe," *American Historical Review*, LI (1946), 419–438.

Swain, J. W., *Edward Gibbon the Historian* (London, 1966).

*Tacitus, *On Britain and Germany*, trans. H. Mattingly (Harmondsworth, Penguin, 1948).   **10, 36, 55**

*———, *The Annals of Imperial Rome*, trans. M. Grant (Harmondsworth, Penguin, 1959).

*Thucydides, *History of the Peloponnesian War*, trans. R. Warner (Harmondsworth, Penguin, 1954).   **9**

Tiraboschi, G., *Storia della Letteratura Italiana* (Modena, 1772–1782), 11 vols.   **23**

Toynbee, A. J., *A Study of History* (London, 1934–1961), 12 vols. **32, 33**

Ullman, B. L., "Leonardo Bruni and Humanist Historiography," *Medievalia et Humanistica*, IV (1946), 45–61.

Usher, A. P., "Soil Fertility, Soil Exhaustion, and Their Historical Significance," *Quarterly Journal of Economics*, XXXVII (1923), 385–411.

Van Werveke, H., "Comment les établissements religieux belges se procuraient-ils du vin au haut moyen âge," *Revue Belge de Philologie et d'Histoire*, II (1923), 643–662.   **75**

*Vasari, *The Lives of the Artists*, trans. G. Bull (Harmondsworth, Penguin, 1965).   **18, 19**

Vasiliev, N. A., *Le problème de la chute de l'empire romain d'Occident et de la civilisation antique* (Kazan, 1921).

Vercauteren, F., "Note sur les rapports entre l'Empire franc et l'Orient à la fin du IXe siècle," *Byzantion*, IV (1927–1928), 434–435.   **61, 75**

———, *Etude sur les civitates de la Belgique seconde* (Brussels, 1934).

Verlinden, C., "L'état économique de l'Alsace sous Louis le Pieux d'après Ermold le Noir," *Revue Belge de Philologie et d'Histoire*, XIII (1934), 166–176.   **73, 75**

———, *L'esclavage dans l'Europe médiévale* (Bruges, 1955), I, 635–728.

Villani, *Croniche Fiorentine*, in L. A. Muratori, *Rerum Italicarum Scriptores* (Milan, 1723–1751), vol. XIII.   **16**

Vogt, J., "Rassenmischung im römische Reich," *Vergangenheit und Gegenwart*, XXVI (1936), 1–11.

Voltaire, *Essai sur les moeurs et l'esprit des nations, et sur les principaux faits de l'histoire, depuis Charlemagne jusqu'à Louis XIII*, in *Oeuvres* (Geneva, 1756), vols. XI–XIII.   **7, 22, 23, 25**

*Walbank, F. W., *The Decline of the Roman Empire in the West* (New York, Schuman, 1953).   **13, 50, 51**

*Wallace-Hadrill, J. M., *The Barbarian West, 400–1000* (New York, Harper Torchbook, 1952).   **64**

Weber, M., *Die sozialen Gründe des Untergangs der antiken Kultur*, in *Gesammelte Aufsätze für Sozial- und Wirtschaftsgeschichte* (Tübingen, 1924).   **49, 50**

Weisinger, H., "The Renaissance Theory of the Reaction Against the Middle Ages as a Cause of the Renaissance," *Speculum*, XX (1945), 461–467.

Westermann, W. L., "The Economic Basis of the Decline of Ancient Culture," *American Historical Review*, XX (1915), 723–743.   **48, 49**

*White, L. T., Jr., *Medieval Technology and Social Change* (Oxford, Galaxy Book, 1962).   **80, 81**

———, (ed.), *The Transformation of the Roman World. Gibbon's Problem After Two Centuries* (Berkeley, 1966).

Index